Trauma-Responsive Strategies for Early Childhood

Trauma-Responsive Strategies for Early Childhood

KATIE STATMAN-WEIL, EDD, LCSW

Redleaf Press®
www.redleafpress.org
800-423-8309

Published by Redleaf Press
10 Yorkton Court
St. Paul, MN 55117
www.redleafpress.org

First edition 2020
Cover design by Erin Kirk New
Interior design by Douglas Schmitz
Typeset in Utopia
Printed in the United States of America
27 26 25 24 23 22 21 20   1 2 3 4 5 6 7 8

Library of Congress Cataloging-in-Publication Data
Names: Statman-Weil, Katie, 1983- author.
Title: Trauma-responsive strategies for early childhood / by Katie
   Statman-Weil.
Description: First edition. | St. Paul, MN : Redleaf Press, 2020. |
   Includes bibliographical references and index. | Summary: "This book
   offers an overview of trauma and its impact on young children, as well
   as specific strategies and techniques educators and administrators can
   use to create classroom and school communities that improve the quality
   of care for children impacted by trauma"-- Provided by publisher.
Identifiers: LCCN 2020010741 (print) | LCCN 2020010742 (ebook) | ISBN
   9781605546636 (paperback) | ISBN 9781605546643 (ebook)
Subjects: LCSH: Early childhood education--Psychological aspects. | Psychic
   trauma in children. | Children with mental disabilities--Education
   (Early childhood) | Children with social disabilities--Education (Early
   childhood) | Classroom environment. | School environment.
Classification: LCC LB1139.23 .S733 2020 (print) | LCC LB1139.23 (ebook)
   | DDC 372.21--dc23
LC record available at https://lccn.loc.gov/2020010741
LC ebook record available at https://lccn.loc.gov/2020010742

Printed on acid-free paper

To my children

You are my greatest joy.

Mothering you is my favorite thing I have ever done.

Contents

Acknowledgments

THIS BOOK WOULD NOT BE POSSIBLE without the support of many people, beginning with those at Redleaf Press who first approached me about writing this book. I am honored to be a Redleaf author.

Over the years, I have had the pleasure of working with many skilled educators, and I would like to offer thanks to each of the dedicated, compassionate, and reflective teachers I have known. You have taught me so much about how to teach and learn alongside young children. I would like to offer a specific thank-you to Stephen, who spent countless hours talking theory and practice with me as both an educator and administrator, and for that I am grateful. I am so glad you were there to carry on Wild Lilac's mission and vision.

To my mom, Leah, and to my dad, Ron: You created a childhood for me that all children deserve. My work with children, families, and teachers is driven by my desire to ensure other young people feel the love and safety I felt as a child. I miss you both terribly.

To my sister, Zoe: Your support of me and my family has been so meaningful. You have embraced the mess and chaos of foster care and adoption and loved all of my children the way they deserve to be loved. Thank you.

To Helene: If we had not decided to join forces in 2006, who knows where I would be now? Certainly not here. I am grateful for your love and unending friendship. We have grown, and we are better, and somehow through all of it, we did that together.

To my partner, Mark: You have made my wildest dreams come true. Your support and love made this book possible. Your countless early mornings caring for our children as they got ready for school gave me the time and space I needed to write. I still cannot believe I was so lucky to have found you.

To my children's families: Thank you for trusting me to love and care for our children. I have learned so much from each of you about how to parent and how to imagine family. There is no greater joy in my life than watching our amazing children grow.

To my children: This book is for you. I am amazed every day by who you are and what you bring to the world. Deja, you are strong and driven, and I cannot wait to watch your story unfold. Moving to Nehalem Street was the best decision we ever made. Akaylee, you are smart, thoughtful, and wise. You are also the best big sister I could ever dream up for the littles. Danielle, your tenacity and strength delight and surprise me every day; watching you be you is the best. Ricardo, your unbelievably happy spirit and quick giggles brighten every day. We had no idea what we were missing until we met you.

Preface

MY VIEW OF TRAUMA AND TRAUMA EXPRESSION is rooted in my personal experience and educational background in both social work and education. At the heart of my practice and my vision for this book is the belief that all of us need relationships and support to thrive; and to create these deep, fulfilling relationships, we must truly see and know each other. My intent is for this book to offer strategies that move beyond simply trying to change behaviors—although behaviors will change or dissipate once children feel safe—and instead allow us to understand how young children's development and behavior are connected to their social worlds and lived experiences. Rather than seeing children's behaviors as the heart of the problem, my hope is that we are instead able to see behavior as a physical manifestation of how children's bodies and brains are reacting to traumatic experiences. Children are telling us through their actions and words how they feel, and our job is to listen.

Children who have experienced early childhood trauma are in our schools and classrooms. Each of us has the power to be a changing force in the lives of these young people who may not yet know that the world can be safe, nurturing, and warm. Children who have experienced early traumas may have big behaviors that demand our attention, or they may be quiet and withdrawn. They may tell us about the trauma they have experienced, or they may act like everything has always been fine at home. They may be working on recovering from the trauma they experienced, or they may still be living in a traumatic environment. No matter what, they need us to be trauma-responsive educators who understand how brain development, attachment, and early learning are all connected.

This book offers the research context to help understand how trauma can disrupt and change children's development and behavior. Once we understand *why* and *how* children are affected by early trauma, I will explore ideas and strategies to support children's healing. As school administrators and educators, we have the potential to offer reparative interactions and trauma-responsive strategies that allow children to heal and grow. Working from a relationship-based framework of connection, understanding, and attunement, I offer a blueprint for creating schools and classrooms that can transform young children's views of themselves and the world around them.

Chapter 1

What Is Trauma?

Mirabelle is five years old. She was recently removed from the care of her grandma—whom she had lived with since birth—after authorities discovered that the grandmother's boyfriend was sexually abusing her. She has been living in a foster home for two and a half months and started kindergarten last week. While it has only been a few weeks, her teacher is already starting to worry. Mirabelle does not join the group for circle time, has a hard time focusing on her school-work, and is refusing to participate in any activity she deems "boring." However, her teacher has noticed that Mirabelle is very social, has already made several friends, and loves recess and free-play time.

Hector is in his second year of preschool and has experienced neglect as well as several disrupted attachments. His mom, who was in recovery when he was born, relapsed and started to use illicit substances again when he was just six months old. Once his extended family found out, his relatives stepped in, and for the next year and a half, Hector was passed from family member to family member for weeks or sometimes months at a time as they tried to keep him out of the foster-care system. However, at two, Hector's mom was arrested and sent to a yearlong drug rehabilitation program. Shortly after she graduated from rehab, Hector was able to move back in with his mom, and the two of them moved into a sober housing unit. Hector's mom is a loving and involved mom now that she is sober and par-ticipates in weekly therapy with him. Hector loves school, but he does not seem to have any strong attachments to any of his teachers. He will just as likely curl up in the lap of a substitute he just met as he will with his two primary teachers, whom he's known for nearly two years. Hector also has a hard time calming down once

he is upset and often demonstrates his big feelings by using his body: he kicks, hits, and even bites to communicate his needs and feelings. He recently threw a block at a teacher's head, which sent her to the hospital for stitches.

🖐 🖐 🖐 🖐 🖐

Zayda is a one-year-old baby who lives with her mom, dad, and two older brothers. Zayda's family has a long history of domestic violence; both of her parents have been arrested multiple times for domestic-violence incidents. The picturesque family they portray to their friends and family is not at all what they are like behind closed doors. Zayda is very shut down and gets overwhelmed by loud noises and quick movements. She attends a full-day child care program three days a week; while there, she hardly ever makes noise and seems content watching other children play all day long. At naptime she does not ever want help falling asleep and instead prefers not to be cuddled or touched. She puts herself to sleep by staring at the ceiling. Her teachers are concerned about her behavior because she often seems to be in her own world, but her parents just describe her as very independent.

🖐 🖐 🖐 🖐 🖐

The greatest hope for traumatized, abused, and neglected children is to receive a good education in schools where they are seen and known, where they learn to regulate themselves, and where they can develop a sense of agency. At their best, schools can function as islands of safety in a chaotic world. They can teach children how their bodies and brains work and how they can understand and deal with their emotions. Schools can play a significant role in instilling the resilience necessary to deal with the traumas of neighborhoods or families. (van der Kolk 2014, 353)

Mirabelle, Hector, and Zayda are just a few examples of the many young children who experience early traumas. Such traumas include emotional, physical, and sexual abuse; neglect, where basic needs are not being met; domestic violence; adoption; foster care; prohibition of gender identity and expression; racial discrimination; incarceration or death of a caregiver; a pandemic; natural disasters;

medical and surgical procedures; serious accidents; and more (Roberts et al. 2012; van der Kolk 2014). In 2018 an estimated 678,000 children experienced abuse and neglect in the United States. Of the children who experienced documented abuse and neglect, 60 percent experienced neglect as a singular form of maltreatment, 10.7 percent experienced physical abuse as a singular maltreatment, and 7 percent experienced sexual abuse as a singular maltreatment. Some children (15.5 percent) experienced more than one type of trauma. More than half were between birth and eight years of age (62.5 percent), with the highest rate of maltreatment being for children younger than one year old (15.3 percent). Over one quarter (28.7 percent) were two years old or younger, 17.8 percent were between the ages of three and five, and 16 percent were between the ages of six and eight. The majority (77.5 percent) of these early traumas were committed by the children's own parents (HHS 2020).

Given these statistics, early childhood educators throughout their careers are likely to teach young children who have experienced trauma. They are in our classrooms and schools, and they need connection and love, just like all other children. Experiencing early trauma influences how children see the world and who they are. Because children's development happens within the context of their earliest experiences, it is vitally important to understand the impact of adversity on young children as they grow.

Definitions of Trauma

Many different forms of trauma can affect young children's experiences and sense of self. Here are some definitions that encompass what will be discussed in this book:

> *Trauma* "results from an event, series of events, or set of circumstances that is experienced by an individual as physically or emotionally harmful or life-threatening with lasting adverse effects on the individual's functioning and mental, physical, social, emotional, or spiritual well-being" (SAMHSA 2014). Trauma is defined by the experience of the survivor; two people can experience the same event and respond psychologically in very different ways.

Acute trauma is a single traumatic event that produces severe emotional or physical distress. Acute traumas include incidents such as a car accident, theft, or witnessing a violent event.

Complex trauma is repeated interpersonal trauma occurring during crucial periods of development. Complex trauma occurs when trauma takes place within the context of children's cognitive, physical, linguistic, social, and emotional development. Complex trauma specifically considers the impact trauma can have on children's brains, development, and successful mastery of milestones. Another more detailed definition of complex trauma describes it as "multiple traumatic events that occur [to children] within the caregiving system—the social environment that is supposed to be the source of safety and stability in a child's life" (Cook et al. 2003, 5). Complex trauma is persistent but often unpredictable and episodic. For example, Mirabelle, who was sexually abused by her grandmother's boyfriend, was subject to a complex trauma; it happened over time and only occurred when her grandmother was not around. Other examples of complex traumas are witnessing domestic violence, experiencing repeated physical abuse, living in a war zone, or living with an individual addicted to drugs or alcohol.

Intergenerational trauma (also known as historical trauma, collective trauma, or community trauma) is a form of collective complex trauma that impacts entire communities and is transmitted across generations. It can be seen in the descendants of trauma survivors whose communities have suffered major traumas or abuses. Some of the communities that have been affected by intergenerational trauma in the United States include the African American community that survived slavery, the indigenous peoples who survived the genocide and displacement of their communities' members, and the descendants of those who survived the Holocaust. A result of this collective trauma is traumatic stress rippling across generations of people (Isobel et al. 2018). Being aware of these legacies and effects of intergenerational trauma is important for caregivers, as it is through this awareness that teachers and administrators can better understand and support the children and families they work with.

Racial trauma (also known as race-based traumatic stress) refers to "emotional or physical pain or the threat of physical and emotional pain that results from racism" (Carter 2007, 88). Racial trauma is often linked to intergenerational trauma, the impact of remembering and dealing with the denigration of one's community, and the ongoing effects of stress due to societal racism (Hemmings and Evans 2017). As the National Child Traumatic Stress Network (2017) explains, "Racial disparities persist in our education system: youth of color have disproportionately lower access to preschool, higher rates of suspension from preschool onward, and limited access to advanced classes and college counselors as compared to their white counterparts" (3). This quantifiable gap in access to resources and the bias experienced by students of color are manifestations of the systemic impact of both historical trauma and racial trauma on communities of color. Connected to both historical and racial trauma is the vast overrepresentation of children of color (and children living in poverty) in the child welfare system, despite the research demonstrating that families of color are no more likely than white families to abuse or neglect their children (Child Welfare Information Gateway 2016). To address racial trauma, schools as institutions, and white teachers and administrators in particular, must acknowledge and understand racism and its effects (Hemmings and Evans 2017; NCTSN 2017).

Trauma-responsive schools are educational environments where teachers and other school personnel are aware of the effects and impact of trauma on young children's brains and development. Trauma-responsive schools are inclusive of all young children and their families and actively modify their environments and curricula depending on who the children are in their classrooms.

The Impact of Trauma on Development

Research shows us that experiencing early trauma can impact brain development in adverse ways. Survivors of childhood trauma are more likely than those who have not experienced trauma to have trouble processing and remembering information, differentiating between safe and unsafe situations, connecting to and trusting adults, and regulating their feelings. Children who lack these skills experience uncertainty and difficulties both socially and academically (Siegel and Payne Bryson 2011).

Typically when children experience overwhelming feelings, they rely on their caregivers to help them feel calm and safe. However, young children who experience unpredictable caregiving or violence in their homes may not have the same positive self-feelings as their securely attached peers. Instead they may develop negative expectations and beliefs about the world and about themselves. Children learn about the world through their caregivers' response to them when they express different emotions. This interaction allows each child to construct what John Bowlby (1980) termed an "internal working model," which refers to the way children internalize the emotional and cognitive characteristics of their primary relationships. Children seek out their caregivers for security and stability, but when their caregivers are the source of their fear or their caregivers are not consistent, they can end up feeling hopeless and out of control. All of their life experiences have led them to view the world as unsafe and threatening, as a place where violence and fear are likely. Like Hector, who experienced multiple caregivers in his early life, children who experience early trauma may not have safe adults to help them learn to regulate their emotional and physical reactions to stressful events, which leaves them ill equipped to navigate the academic and social dimensions of school (SAMHSA 2014). This also leaves young trauma survivors at risk for being overwhelmed by feelings of distress and unable to regulate their emotional and physical responses to their feelings (van der Kolk 2014).

Children who experience complex traumas may not realize that they see the world differently than their peers, because theirs is the only reality they know. They do not walk into school assuming things will be different from how they have been at home. Instead they come into our classrooms with their unique understanding of how the world works. If home is a scary and painful place, then they naturally assume that school is a scary and painful place. Thus children who have experienced early violence and fear may spend their time at school on high alert for danger because they are understandably working to keep themselves safe. Unfortunately, their need to focus on physical and emotional safety can keep them from developing both their academic and social capacities (van der Kolk 2014).

With the case of Mirabelle, her safe and predictable world was shattered when she was sexually abused by her grandmother's boyfriend, and was replaced by a world where her body was no longer guaranteed to be safe. Mirabelle's behaviors in the classroom are not coming from a place of defiance or even boredom but rather a place of survival. Her world has become overloaded with difficult feelings, and her inability to focus is in fact her way of coping with these overpowering emotions. Mirabelle is constantly scanning the room for danger as a way of keeping herself safe and managing her stress. It is a survival mechanism that, while adaptive in some contexts, becomes maladaptive when it overrides everyday experiences, as it has for Mirabelle.

Fight, Flight, or Freeze: The Stress Response

Children who live in unpredictable and scary environments may have brains that are shaped to expect uncertainty and fear. Research demonstrates that our brains are wired to respond to threats to our mental and physical safety by initiating a series of chemical and neurological activity—known as the *stress response*—that triggers our biological instinct to fight, flee, or freeze (van der Kolk 2014).

Imagine for a moment that you are taking a peaceful walk down by a river, and all of a sudden you see in front of you a mama crocodile and her hatchlings. Your brain perceives an immediate threat: that crocodile is going to do everything in her power to protect her babies, and you just got a little too close. Your brain automatically understands the need to protect yourself and goes into survival mode. Rather than stopping to think, *Wow, this is surprising—I wasn't expecting to see a crocodile by this river!* your brain is primed to respond immediately to the threat. Your brain instantly sends out the signals to release stress hormones, and your body gets ready to either fight that mama crocodile, run from that mama crocodile, or freeze so as not to threaten that mama crocodile. Evolution has taught your brain and body how to work together to keep you safe in this dangerous situation, and these instincts can save your life when you come face-to-face with a crocodile. Problems arise, however, when that croco-dile is not a once-in-a-lifetime experience but rather an everyday experience at home. When the crocodile is actually a caregiver who is a constant threat in your daily life, your stress-response system goes into overdrive and is activated over and over again, transforming it from a healthy and lifesaving tool your brain uses to keep you safe into something that harms healthy brain development (van der Kolk 2014).

Fight, Flight, or Freeze

The body has three common responses to stress: the fight, flight, and freeze instincts. These are defined as follows.

Fight: aggression, oppositional behavior, hyperactivity, and constant or impul-sive movement
Some of the behaviors we see in children in fight mode include the following:

- yelling or screaming

- cursing

- arguing

- threatening people

- physical violence such as hitting, kicking, biting, spitting, scratching, or head-butting other children or adults

- throwing and destroying materials and the environment

Flight: running away, avoidance of conflict, and social isolation
Some of the behaviors we see in children in flight mode include the following:

- physically trying to disappear by covering their faces with their hands, pulling their jackets or hats over their faces, covering themselves with a blanket, and so forth

- hiding in the classroom or school

- running out of the classroom or school

- going under the table or chairs to get away from others

- becoming engrossed in an activity and appearing unaware of others, particu-larly when there have been upsetting conversations, noises, or events

- sitting and watching the classroom activities without participating

Freeze: withdrawal, daydreaming, being ultra-quiet, forgetfulness, hyper-compliance, and emotional numbing

Some of the behaviors we see in children in freeze mode include the following:

- appearing to daydream a lot
- seeming lethargic or zoned out
- having a flat or blank look on their faces with little facial expression
- eyes looking glazed over
- being unresponsive to any sort of engagement, such as questions, games, smiles, calling the child's name, and so forth
- falling asleep when things are loud, chaotic, or unfamiliar
- not engaging with toys or materials

Triggers

A trigger is something a child sees, hears, feels, or smells that is a reminder of a past trauma. When children who have experienced trauma encounter a trigger, it is as if there is a current physical or emotional threat, so those children respond in a way that protects themselves (NCTSN 2014).

Possible triggers in the classroom include the following:

- changes to the classroom environment
- loud noises
- transitions
- new children or adults
- turning the lights on or off
- fast movements
- being bumped or touched
- certain smells
- certain sounds
- hearing specific words or phrases

- a change in schedule

- unpredictable schedules

- seeing or hearing another child be upset

- seeing an adult upset or frustrated

- mealtimes

- naptime

- drop-off or pickup transitions

- a toy or other item being taken away

- a change in teacher or a teacher being absent without warning

- disorganized or messy classroom environments

Children are particularly sensitive to the repeated activation of this stress response because their brains and bodies are still developing (Siegel and Payne Bryson 2011). Repeated trauma, and thus the repeated activation of the stress response, affects the brain's structure and can impact every aspect of young children's development. As a result, rather than being a constructive tool that helps children stay safe, the stress response can cause a child to be in a constant state of hyperarousal, so even when danger is not present, they may act as though it is. This can cause children to live in a continuous state of fear, which means that to protect themselves, they are constantly on alert for threats and are always at the ready to fight, flee, or freeze when faced with perceived dangers, like Zayda, who perpetually shuts down in a "freeze" response as a means of protection. These responses can inhibit children's higher-level thinking and their ability to learn in the classroom environment (Siegel and Payne Bryson 2011).

Contemporary research demonstrates that trauma in early childhood can be a factor in many mental and physical health issues. Along with neurobiological changes, early trauma can have negative behavioral, emotional, and developmental repercussions throughout children's schooling and adult lives. Children who experience complex trauma have higher rates of school absences and are three times more likely to drop out of school than their peers. They score lower on standardized tests and have lower GPAs and decreased reading abilities. They also have higher rates of suspension and expulsion and are more likely to be placed in special-education classrooms (NCTSN 2014). These poor academic outcomes for children who have experienced maltreatment have been demonstrated across a variety of trauma exposures (for example, physical and sexual abuse, neglect, or exposure to interpersonal violence) and cannot be explained through other psychosocial stressors, such as experiencing poverty. Along with these poor academic outcomes, those who experience chronic childhood adversity are more likely to grow up to experience physical and mental health issues, criminal activity, and substance use and abuse (Felitti et al. 1998; van der Kolk 2014).

Children who have survived trauma may experience impairments across their development, which can cause difficult and troubling behaviors in the classroom (Child Welfare Information Gateway 2014a). Healthy development is often connected to the attachment relationships children have with their caregivers. Without nurturing and attuned early connections, children's development is typically interrupted and thrown into chaos. This leads to some children who have experienced trauma having irregular developmental patterns, where some developmental domains (such as cognitive, language, physical, or social-emotional development) may be overdeveloped while others are woefully underdeveloped. Thus the experiences children have prior to entering the classroom directly influence who and how they are in the classroom community. Their ability to function—their normal—has everything to do with their earliest experiences. Therefore, when supporting children who have challenging and erratic behaviors, we must remember that they are expressing what they know *at that moment*. We must meet them where they are if we hope to be able to support them in growing and changing.

Symptoms and Behaviors Connected to Children Who Have Experienced Trauma

Children, particularly young children, often communicate through their bodies more than through their words. To be attuned and connected trauma-responsive educators, it is important for us to recognize some of the symptoms and behaviors children who have experienced trauma may express. These symptoms and behaviors should not be construed as negative descriptors of the children themselves, as will be discussed in chapter 2—children's brains and bodies change in response to trauma. Their behaviors have adapted based on their early experiences of adversity. It is our job as educators to recognize trauma symptoms and respond to them with the compassion and relationship-based techniques that children need to heal (Child Welfare Information Gateway 2014a). Outlined below are some of the reactions young children may have to early trauma:

Infants:

- **Needing closeness/separation anxiety.** Infants may not feel comfortable moving away from their caregiver to explore the environment, which can constrict their play and hinder their curiosity. They may want to be held or be close to their caregiver throughout the day. They may have extreme separation anxiety and not be able to be soothed when their primary caregiver leaves.

- **Easily startled.** Babies who have experienced early adversity may startle easily and seem to be constantly on edge.

- **Uncomfortable with touch.** Infants may not want touch and may arch their backs or scream if they are held closely. They may throw themselves backward out of their caregiver's arms or continue to move around so they do not settle into their caregiver. Older babies may pull hair or scratch to get away from the caregiver holding them.

- **Hard to soothe.** Babies may be difficult to soothe and constantly fussy. Babies exposed to substances in utero may have a shrill and persistent cry.

- **Lack of smiles, coos, and interaction.** Babies may have a hard time connecting to others through direct, playful interaction. Typically babies show their emotions to express their needs and wants; however, infants who have experienced trauma may be shut down from their emotions and may be described as "serious," "numb," or "distant." Zayda, who witnesses domestic violence in her home, often shuts down at child care as a way of protecting herself from the loud noises and hurried movements that can occur in the classroom setting. Babies as young as four months old can show signs of depression.

- **Glossed-over eyes.** Infants will turn their eyes away from their care-givers, look past their caregivers as if they are looking at something beyond them, or seem to look through their caregivers rather than at them. Their eyes may look glossy and blank.

- **Sleep disturbances.** Infants may have a hard time falling asleep or staying asleep and be easily awoken. Conversely, they may sleep so deeply that nothing seems to wake them.

- **Challenges with eating.** Babies who have experienced trauma may have trouble latching on to bottles. They may spit up often and have sensitive stomachs.

- **Developmental regressions.** Children may lose developmental milestones they have already mastered. For example, they may lose the ability to crawl or sit up, or they may stop cooing or babbling.

- **Physical expression of big feelings.** Because self-regulation is learned through coregulation, babies who experience early trauma, particularly relational trauma, may have a hard time managing big feelings. They may cry and scream much longer than other infants when upset. They may express big feelings through behavior such as excessive rocking, head banging, and slapping or biting themselves.

Toddlers:

- **Needing closeness/separation anxiety.** Like infants, toddlers who have experienced trauma may try to keep themselves safe by staying close to their caregivers and may have difficulty separating from their primary caregivers in the morning as they enter the classroom. They may be fearful of trying new activities and ask for lots of help for activities they are developmentally capable of completing on their own.

- **Easily startled.** Toddlers may be easily startled by loud noises, new faces, and minor behavioral corrections.

- **Hard to soothe.** Toddlers who have experienced trauma may not want comfort when they are upset or get hurt; they may feel like they must take care of their feelings on their own without adult support. Feelings may feel shameful to them and be something they want to hide.

- **Sleep disturbances.** Toddlers may have a hard time falling asleep or staying asleep, or they may sleep so deeply that nothing seems to wake them.

- **Challenges with eating.** Toddlers may have aversions to certain textures and tastes. The diagnosis of "failure to thrive" can sometimes be connected to relationship-based trauma. Conversely, they may always seem hungry and eat too fast or too much, which can result in choking or throwing up their food.

- **Developmental regression.** Regression occurs when children return to an earlier stage of behavior or physical development. Toddlers may lose skills they had previously mastered, such as the ability to use the toilet, take clothes on and off, or climb.

- **Developmental delays.** Toddlers may experience physical, cognitive, and social-emotional delays. Toddlers who have experienced trauma may not have the language skills their peers possess, and it may take them a long time to process what is said to them.

- **Physical expression of big feelings.** Like infants, toddlers may have a hard time managing big feelings. They may cry and scream much longer than typically expected when upset. They may express big feelings through behavior such as excessive rocking, head banging, and slapping or biting themselves. They may be physically aggressive toward peers and adults. They may escalate quickly out of seemingly nowhere.

- **Withdrawal.** Toddlers may be overwhelmed by their big feelings and learn to cope by withdrawing into themselves and shutting themselves off from their emotions and the world around them. They may spend most of their time by themselves and seldom interact with their peers or teachers.

- **Inconsistent play.** Toddlers typically enjoy play that involves learning how the world works, such as moving items from one place to another, dumping and pouring, and pushing things with wheels around the floor. However, toddlers who have experienced trauma may have unpredictable play that seems to have little purpose. They may act as if they are constantly looking for a way to enter or engage in play. They may walk over to other children engaged in play and watch them for a few moments before moving on to another child or another activity. They are in constant motion without moving anywhere or to anything.

- **Irritability, negativity, or sadness.** Anxiety and depression can both be expressed as irritability or negativity. Often toddlers who do not have the words to put to their big feelings will express dislike or distaste for activities through irritability, negativity, or sadness.

Three- to Five-Year-Olds:

- **Needing closeness/separation anxiety.** Like infants and toddlers, preschoolers may want to stay near their teachers for most of the day. They may be fearful of trying new things and ask for help for tasks they are developmentally capable of completing on their own. They may have a hard time separating from their caregiver when they arrive at school and may take a long time to reregulate after that separation.

- **Hard to soothe.** Like toddlers, preschoolers who have experienced trauma may not want comfort when they are upset or get hurt. They may feel like they must take care of their feelings on their own, without adult support. Feelings may be shameful to them and something they want to hide.

- **Challenges with eating.** Like toddlers, children may have aversions to certain textures and tastes. They may always seem hungry and eat too fast or too much, which can result in choking or throwing up their food. They may fear they will not be fed regularly, even when they are living in an environment that does feed them regularly. To ensure they always have enough, they may take food from other children or hide food in their clothing or cubbies for later.

- **Attachment difficulties.** Children who have had a lot of caregiver inconsistency in their early lives may not behave differently with different adults, as we would expect with healthy attachment. Like Hector, who was passed between family members in his early years, they may climb into the laps of new substitute teachers or family members of other children as if they have known them their whole lives. They may run up and hug strangers or seek out people they do not know to help them complete tasks like putting on their shoes or jackets.

- **Overly developed capacity for self-care.** Children who have been neglected may learn at an early age to care for themselves and others. They may be capable of making themselves meals and changing their young siblings' diapers but not have the developmentally typical capacity to name colors or shapes.

- **Hypervigilance.** Preschoolers who have lived or live in unpredictable and stressful environments may have a hard time calming themselves and focusing because they are constantly scanning the environment for threats to their physical and emotional safety. This can make preschoolers seem inattentive, impulsive, and hyperactive.

- **Difficulty with peer and adult relationships.** Preschoolers may have trouble playing and interacting with their peers. They may be unintentionally rough, aggressive, or oppositional with their peers and teachers. Small disagreements or accidents with friends may feel like huge breaches of safety to preschoolers who have experienced trauma. Their behaviors may seem controlling, manipulative, or sneaky when in fact they are using adaptive behaviors to keep themselves emotionally and physically safe. They may be emotionally distant in the classroom, or they may be extremely clingy.

- **Developmental regression.** Preschoolers who experience trauma may regress in their abilities. They may have toileting accidents, seem to lose language, or return to needing to carry around a comfort object with them.

- **Developmental delays.** Preschoolers who experience complex trauma may experience delays across the developmental domains. By preschool their developmental age may be noticeably different from their chronological age. They may need the supports of younger children to feel safe and nurtured.

- **Restricted or repetitive play.** Preschoolers who have experienced early adversity may find play challenging. They may have a hard time concentrating, negotiating, problem solving, and moving into an imaginative world. They may replay traumatic events and get stuck in overwhelming emotions.

- **Somatic complaints.** Preschoolers may experience stomachaches or headaches or complain of severe pain when they get bumps or scrapes. Conversely, the opposite may be true, and they may not articulate when they have serious injuries or illnesses.

- **Sexualized behavior.** Exploring bodies and private parts with others is typical for young children. However, children who have experienced sexual trauma may move beyond simple exploration and try to replay their trauma in the classroom. They may talk about or act out sex acts that are clearly beyond their developmental level (such as a three-year-old trying to kiss a teacher's genitals). They may ask other children to keep "secrets" about sexual exploration they are doing in hidden places.

- **Talking about the traumatic event.** Children may incessantly talk about the traumas they have experienced as a way of calming themselves and understanding the traumas they have experienced.

- **Challenges with transitions.** Preschoolers may have a hard time transitioning from one activity to another. They may fear the unknown, and transition times may bring up big feelings and behaviors in an effort to control the unpredictability of switching activities.

- **Memory challenges.** Preschoolers who have experienced complex trauma may have challenges with their short-term memories. They often will not remember the tasks they are supposed to complete next. When a teacher says to a child, "Please go get your boots and your jacket and bring them over to me," the child may run off to grab their boots and jacket but be found ten minutes later still by their cubby. This sort of scenario is often seen as noncompliance when in fact it is simply not remembering what they were supposed to do next.

Six- to Eight-Year-Olds:

- **Challenges with eating.** School-aged children who have experienced food insecurity may hoard or gorge on food, and this may result in them throwing up or having chronic stomachaches. They may store food in their pockets or backpacks for later or take food from other children. This behavior is often seen as stealing; however, it is important to recognize it as an adaptive strategy to ensure the children receive the nutrients they need. Children may also eat very little or be picky eaters, avoiding certain textures or food groups.

- **Developmental delays.** School-aged children who experience complex trauma may experience developmental delays in a variety of areas. In the elementary classroom, language delays and behavioral challenges are often the first things noticed. However, children may have delays across the developmental domains. These delays can cause challenges in a structured and academically rigorous school environment.

- **Difficulty conforming to school norms.** Young elementary students who have experienced early adversity may have delays in their social-emotional and behavioral development that lead to challenges complying with behavioral expectations in the classroom. Children may appear demanding, inflexible, controlling, or oppositional, when really these behaviors are all adaptive measures to keep themselves safe. These children may be hypervigilant and have a hard time concentrating on academic tasks. They may be seen as lying, stealing, or manipulating to get what they want; it is vitally important that we see these behaviors as results of early trauma, not an indication of the children's characters.

- **Trouble regulating.** Children who experience trauma may have a hard time regulating their emotions and being flexible in their thinking. Often their big reactions (for example, sobbing when someone cuts in front of them at the water fountain) to what adults consider small problems leads to their feelings being dismissed. They may be described as oppositional, combative, irritable, negative, easily frustrated, or emotionally distant and withdrawn. These are all labels that miss the underlying issue, which is that children who experience trauma may have adaptive biological changes that are put into place to ensure their safety. To support regulation, we must first offer interventions based on building safe and trusting relationships and helping children heal from the trauma they have experienced, rather than on punishments.

- **Hypervigilance.** Like preschoolers, six- to eight-year-olds who have lived in unpredictable and stressful environments may find it challenging to remain calm and focus on academic work because they are overly alert to danger.

- **Easily startled, or not.** Elementary-age children who have survived trauma may be triggered by reminders of those experiences. They may be jumpy or easily startled by unexpected noises or movements, such as clapping, school bells, or having someone unexpectedly touch them. The opposite may also be true; some children are desensitized to the point that they hardly notice unexpected noises or movements.

- **Challenges in play.** Children may not have the social-emotional and language skills to problem-solve and negotiate with their peers. For these children, recess and lunchtime may be challenging when there is less support from adults and children are expected to manage their behaviors on their own.

- **Somatic complaints.** Like preschoolers, young elementary students may experience stomachaches and headaches or complain of severe pain when they get bumps or scrapes. The opposite may also be true, and some children may not articulate when they have serious injuries or illnesses.

- **Needing lots of help.** Children who have experienced trauma may ask for help more than other children; they may simply need more attention and closeness from their teachers, or they may need support in learning they are capable of doing things on their own.

- **Sexualized behavior.** Early elementary–age students may talk about sexual acts or pretend to act out sex acts at school that are beyond their developmental level. While body exploration is typical and healthy, when the activity becomes the sole focus of play and interferes with other interests and activities or involves threats, force, or aggression, it is an issue that needs to be addressed.

■ **Change in mood and behavior.** Elementary-age children who experience trauma may have changes in their mood and show signs of sadness or depression. They may be listless and disengaged from their schoolwork, or on the other hand, they may be more active and have angry or aggressive outbursts.

■ **Sleepy or tired in class.** Children may be tired or seem sleepy in class because they are having trouble sleeping at home due to current violence or memories of past trauma. They may experience bad dreams or nightmares, which may make them not want to fall asleep or have a hard time falling asleep.

■ **Overly developed capacity for self-care.** Children who have experienced neglect may find that by elementary school, they are being tasked with caring for their younger siblings in a parenting role. In these neglectful situations, children may be left home to care for their siblings for days or even weeks at a time, which is very different from families where the caregiving adults are active and present in children's lives and also rely on support and help from older siblings. Children in neglectful situations may learn at an early age to care for themselves and others. They may learn to hide what is happening at home as they learn tasks above their developmental level.

■ **Challenges with transitions.** Change can be scary and overwhelming for children who have experienced trauma. Patterns often develop where children's behavior escalates during transitional periods during the day: moving from one activity to another, from the classroom to another part of the school, or from recess or lunch back to the classroom. Transitions can cause anxiety and worry for students, which is often perceived as defiance, aggression, or clowning around.

■ **Memory challenges.** Elementary-age children may have challenges with short- and long-term memory. They may not be able to remember the basic classroom routines and may need more reminders than their peers. They may have challenges holding new academic concepts in their brains over time and will need lots of repetition. Children with memory issues are often seen as not complying with their teachers' requests and considered to have behavioral problems, when in fact the children simply do not remember the requests.

Diagnoses Connected to Trauma

Because children's development can be changed by the early traumas they experience, young children may come into the classroom with a formal trauma-related mental health disorder diagnosis. Professionals trained to understand symptoms and current diagnoses accepted within the psychological community determine these diagnoses. Post-traumatic stress disorder (PTSD) is a primary diagnosis connected to trauma symptoms within the Diagnostic and Statistical Manual of Mental Disorders 5 (DSM-5). However, the PTSD diagnosis was created for an adult population, meaning it often does not reflect the true symptoms observed in children who have experienced trauma. Therefore students may come into the classroom with a variety of diagnoses that capture the symptoms of trauma. These diagnoses may include depression, attention-deficit hyperactivity disorder, oppositional defiant disorder, conduct disorder, anxiety disorder, and more (Child Welfare Information Gateway 2014a). These alternative diagnoses can sometimes confuse and muddle the impact of trauma on children's behaviors and often do not capture the true picture of what has happened in the children's lives. Therefore it is extremely important that we recognize and respond to the expressions of trauma in our classroom rather than simply responding to the clinical diagnosis of a child.

Developmental Domains That Can Be Impaired by Trauma

The symptoms and behaviors we see in young children occur because of disruptions and delays in typical development. The traumas that take place in early childhood can negatively impact attachment and cause changes to children's biology and development. The symptoms and behaviors that follow the traumatic experiences outlined earlier in this chapter are caused by delays or gaps in the following domains: cognitive, language, physical, social-emotional, and academic (Thomason and Marusak 2017; van der Kolk 2014). A gap in any developmental area can cause challenges, and unfortunately these challenges often present as behavioral issues. How well children do in school is connected to how their unique developmental needs are seen and responded to in the classroom environment.

Children's traumatic experiences can have a profound effect on their academic performance. Building early literacy and math skills, which are predictive factors for later school success, requires young children to have the ability to engage effectively in the classroom environment. If a child's experience with trauma makes it difficult or impossible for them to engage with their teacher or the schoolwork, they may not be able to develop these crucial skills.

Seeing Trauma

Understanding that the intensity and expression of children's trauma responses are deeply impacted by their social context is vital. The trauma symptoms we see in a child are impacted not only by the severity of the traumatic event itself and the individual's specific strengths and resiliency factors but also by the response the child receives from their community. If children do not receive adequate support from the people in their communities—whether from family members, teachers, social workers, religious leaders, or other individuals—this can exacerbate their isolation and the effects of their trauma. If, on the other hand, they receive love and trauma-responsive support, this can help them heal from the trauma experienced. This is what trauma specialist Mary Harvey (1996) describes as an "ecological fit," when the surrounding community offers wraparound supports that "reduce isolation, foster social competence, support positive coping, and promote belongingness" (7). When there is an ecological fit between children and their communities, the children fare better.

All classrooms are social and cultural spaces that can reproduce inequities or fight for social change. Our schools, and their teachers and administrators, are huge parts of our children's communities. It is our job as educators to challenge schools to transform into inclusive and supportive educational environments for all learners. To effectively work with children who have experienced trauma, we must acknowledge the institutionalized racism and classism that permeate our school environments and the way this affects how we see and work with children. What teachers perceive as challenging and what diverges from typical social-emotional development is often biased and disproportionately targets children of color and children living in poverty (NCTSN 2017). For example, rates of child maltreatment in community samples are typically similar across ethnic and racial groups. However, African American and Native American children and children of two or more races are overrepresented in foster care and the child welfare system as compared to their representation in the US population in general and among those experiencing poverty (Child Welfare Information Gateway 2016).

Not surprisingly, the implicit and explicit racial and economic biases prevalent within American society (see Carter et al. 2017) permeate the classrooms and experiences of the youngest children. Negative and stereotypical views of children based on race, ethnicity, and socioeconomic status can hinder students' development and negatively affect the ways in which students see themselves as learners and as individuals (Gilliam et al. 2016). For example, a study conducted by Auwarter and Aruguete (2008) found that teachers were more likely to develop negative attitudes about children in lower socioeconomic brackets than their peers from higher socioeconomic bracket families. Furthermore, while poverty can be a risk factor for all children regardless of race, students of color may also need to contend with racial stereotypes and negative beliefs held by teachers. Being a member of a historically marginalized racial or ethnic group often negatively influences the ways in which teachers perceive and respond to students (Gilliam et al. 2016).

For example, a study completed at the Yale Child Study Center by Gilliam, Maupin, Reyes, Accavitti, and Shic (2016) found that both black and white teachers perceive the behavior of black children as more challenging and severe than their white peers. Further, the researchers found that when teachers were given clarifying information about a disruptive child's family stressors and home life, teachers only responded empathetically when the teacher's race matched that of the disruptive student; otherwise they tended to continue to rate the student's behavior more severely than their peers. To create trauma-responsive schools, our school systems must first acknowledge the harm that has been done and is currently being done to marginalized and oppressed communities and the ways that our implicit biases affect how we respond to children's behaviors.

Trauma-Responsive Schools and Classrooms

Although the statistics show that a significant number of children are subject to adverse childhood experiences and that the effects of trauma can be profound, research indicates that a supportive school environment can temper the effects of trauma (Holmes et al. 2014). Trauma-responsive environments ensure that all young children and their families, regardless of abilities, have access to and participate in the schools, with accommodations to environments and curriculum for children whose abilities require them. Creating and maintaining trauma-responsive schools requires commitment to inclusivity from all involved; from the administration to the teachers to the janitors, everyone must believe trauma-responsive environments are necessary and possible.

Trauma-responsive schools and classrooms are spaces where teachers and other adults understand the effects trauma can have on the brain, relationships, and learning. They work in connection to and in support of children and their families. In trauma-responsive classrooms, teachers know that behavior changes through connection and relationships rather than punishments and shame. Teachers create warm and nurturing environments that provide emotional and physical safety so that children can learn new ways of experiencing and seeing themselves and the people around them.

Trauma-responsive schools are built on the foundational belief that children are inherently worthy and capable. To see all children as deserving of supportive environments, all teachers must understand their own biases and recognize the differences between challenging behaviors and culturally bound behaviors. Only when teachers' biases are acknowledged and countered in the classroom can teachers accurately and successfully respond to and serve the children in their classrooms. Teachers must differentiate and offer children varied experiences. Some children need more specialized supports than others; by offering adaptations and individualized responses for our students, we can ensure that all children receive the education they deserve and need to thrive.

Trauma-responsive schools use nonpunitive guidance methods and curricula that counter the expectations and lived experiences of trauma survivors (Holmes et al. 2014). These schools actively work against more traditional educational models that rely on punitive responses to unwanted behaviors. Punitive reactions to children's trauma symptoms can cause them to enter a state of hyperarousal in which they are overwhelmed by emotion and likely to experience a traumatic rather than healing response, which simply reinforces their negative internal working models. Through reparative and healing responses, children learn to see the world in a different way. Offering this alternative experience can fundamentally shift what children believe about the world and who they are.

Schools that are successfully trauma responsive see children within their social contexts and engage their community resources. Teachers within these schools work to be connected to the individual children, their families, and important community supports. They are successful because they offer both individualized support in the classroom and support to the whole family. Families are seen as allies rather than adversaries, and teachers and families work in partnership.

Teachers are capable and powerful change-makers who have the capacity to transform the way children experience and react to the world around them. Trauma-responsive teachers view supporting children's social-emotional development as a deeply important *part of* learning rather than as an *obstacle to* learning.

It is crucial that our schools transform into trauma-responsive spaces where educators have the skills and supports necessary to help children learn new ways of being. Creating trauma-responsive schools can support educators in meeting the diverse needs of all children—including both trauma survivors and their nontraumatized peers.

Conclusion

Developmental trauma—trauma that takes place during childhood—shapes learning. It shapes how children who have experienced trauma see the world, interact with the world, and trust in the world. For educators it is vitally important to take their experiences into account when we plan our curriculum and form our beliefs about who they are and what they are capable of. Only through understanding the profound effects of trauma can we begin to create early childhood education environments that support our youngest learners.

Experiencing developmental trauma can lead to many challenging and disruptive behaviors that negatively influence children's lives. Violence, criminality, and substance use are common outcomes for those who do not receive healthy early experiences; issues that originate in early childhood underpin many of the physical and mental health problems found in adults (Felitti et al. 1998; Hemmings and Evans 2017). However, contemporary trauma research demonstrates that schools can profoundly influence the outcomes for students who have experienced trauma. Thus it is imperative that schools and classrooms become trauma informed and trauma responsive so we can work to meet the needs of all children in our classrooms.

Chapter 2

Brain Development and Attachment

RECENT RESEARCH HAS DRAMATICALLY CHANGED the way we see early brain development. Until the 1980s, many believed that the structure of babies' brains was genetically determined by the time of their births; babies were who they were going to be, and the role of caregivers was solely to nurture their becoming. However, thanks to advancements in neuroimaging technologies, researchers have a new lens with which to view brain development. We now know that children's earliest experiences, both with caregivers and their environment, greatly influence the development of their brain architecture, which is foundational for all future learning, behavior, and health. Both gene expression and environmental experiences affect typical brain development, and the disruption of either one can change the brain dramatically (De Bellis and Zisk 2014).

Although much is still unknown about the brain and the exact ways trauma influences young children, what we do know can go a long way toward helping us understand the young children in our classrooms. Trauma can and does influence the ways in which young children's brains develop and how they see and respond to the world around them. However, brain research also shows that healthy, reparative interactions with educators can and do counter the traumas young children experience outside of school. Using contemporary brain research to create trauma-responsive schools, we can offer young children transformative experiences that allow for healing and growth.

🖐 🖐 🖐 🖐 🖐

When Lorenzo was born, his mom Sara was just sixteen years old. Her family pressured her to place him for adoption, which she did after realizing she would have no familial support if she chose to parent him. Lorenzo's mom chose to have an open adoption, in which she would still get to have a relationship with him as he grew. Lorenzo's adoptive parents, Linda and Bill, have been as loving and supportive as parents could be, and they adore him. Lorenzo is now seven, and Sara recently married and had another baby, whom she is parenting. All of a sudden, Lorenzo's world has felt very unsure, and he has had a lot of questions about his adoption and his place within his family. He has recently started to feel like perhaps he was just not good enough to keep, even though his first mom and adoptive parents all say they love him very much. In school Lorenzo always tries to shine; he wants to be the very best at everything he does, and if he believes he will not succeed, he just will not try a new activity. His teacher is starting to worry he is not pushing himself academically because of his deep fear of failure and his worry that he will not be good enough.

🖐 🖐 🖐 🖐 🖐 🖐

The Developing Brain

In the past, caregivers and practitioners attempted to explain trauma using psychological and behavioral descriptors. However, a growing body of research offers biological explanations for what happens to young children when they experience trauma. Recent research demonstrates that the brain development of children who have experienced early abuse and neglect can be altered and impaired by these early experiences (De Bellis and Zisk 2014). Children's brain development is shaped by their earliest experiences. Neural development and social interactions are deeply connected and can influence how children develop and grow (Badenoch 2008; Siegel and Payne Bryson 2011). The emerging research reveals that both nature and nurture influence development. Although Lorenzo has always been loved, his deep loss at birth has shaped his development more than his parents and his teacher realize. While Lorenzo cannot recall this early memory of losing his first bond and attachment, his body remembers it. As a newborn, he had to form entirely new attachments and trust that his new attachment figures—his adoptive parents, Linda and Bill—would not leave him.

While genetics predispose children to develop in particular ways, the environment in which a child is raised and their early experiences have significant influence on how those genes are expressed. As a result, young children's development is influenced by the multilayered and interlocking personal as well as societal factors that ultimately determine what happens to a child and who they become (De Bellis and Zisk 2014).

Brain Architecture and Development

Babies' brains begin to develop before birth and continue their development into adulthood. When a baby is born, the basic structure of the brain has been formed, although a considerable amount of growth occurs during the early years of a child's life. The architecture of the brain is built sequentially from the "bottom up," moving from simpler functions to more complex ones. The brain is organized as a hierarchy, starting with the brainstem and the midbrain, which regulate the basic bodily functions that are necessary for survival. These lower portions of the brain are quite developed at birth. The higher brain regions—such as the limbic system, which regulates emotion, and the cortex, which allows for complex thinking and abstract thought—develop rapidly after birth. The different areas of the brain complete their functions through multifaceted and complex processes that allow for the transmission of information between areas of the brain and the body (Child Welfare Information Gateway 2015; Siegel and Payne Bryson 2011).

Just as the brain develops vertically, it also forms horizontally, with a left side and a right side. Each side has its own role, vastly different from the other, and the brain only functions as expected when the two sides work together. The left side of the brain governs logical thinking and organizes experiences and thoughts. The right side of the brain helps with emotional expression and reading nonverbal cues (Siegel and Payne Bryson 2011). Young children rely heavily on their right brain, as early development is centered around emotions and relationships.

Many of us have heard the old adage "use it or lose it," which aptly describes what occurs during early brain development. The areas of our brains that are used the most are the ones that develop the most. Because brain development is still a burgeoning field, there is still much more to learn about how trauma affects the brain, but there are certain areas that we know are influenced by early stressful and traumatic experiences.

Brains are made up of nerve cells, called neurons. During fetal development, neurons are created and migrate to form the different parts of the brain. As neurons move, they also become specialized for the area of the brain they regulate. Newborns' brains have over one hundred billion neurons, which constitute almost all the neurons they will have throughout their entire lives. Brain architecture is formed through the billions of neural connections, made across the different parts of the brain (Budday, Steinmann, and Kuhl 2014). During babies' first few years of life, more than one million new neural connections, called synapses, are made every second. As this action is often described, neurons that fire together wire together, meaning the architecture of our brains is shaped by the experiences we have. Therefore the more of the same type of experiences we have, the more we will come to expect those experiences in our lives (Siegel and Payne Bryson 2011).

Children's neurons and neural connections must be exercised for their brains to develop to their full potential. As a child grows, the brain develops and becomes larger and denser as these different neuronal growth processes occur. By three years old, a child's brain has grown to 90 percent of its adult size (Child Welfare Information Gateway 2015). What is key to understanding trauma is that brain growth is dependent on early experiences. Along with genetics, a child's experiences and the frequency of those experiences determine which neural connections are strengthened and expanded and which connections are lost through pruning, the process by which unnecessary, damaged, or degraded neurons are discarded (Budday, Steinmann, and Kuhl 2014).

Without use, brain regions will not grow. While most neural connections are forged during the first three years, new connections can be made and neurons can be pruned throughout one's life. The early connections made offer either a strong or weak base for the connections that come later in life, as connections beget connections (Child Welfare Information Gateway 2015). Children's brains prepare them to expect certain experiences based on what they have experienced before; neural pathways are created based on stimulation of specific regions of the brain. For instance, the more young children hear language, the more the regions of their brain that control speech and language are stimulated, which leads to organization within that part of the brain. If children are not exposed to language-rich environments, the pathways that are developed with the prospect of speech and language may be pruned, making the development of language more challenging. For example, take Ruby, an eight-year-old third grader who has grown up in a household with little stimulation or adult interaction. She has been primarily raised by her twelve-year-old brother because her parents are often gone for long stretches of time. While Ruby is of average intelligence, she often struggles in class because she is simply missing some of the language her peers seem to know. For instance, Ruby's teacher was reading a book aloud that involved the characters visiting the bank of a river, but since Ruby had no idea what the bank of a river was, and she could not imagine how a building that holds money and a river were connected, the chapter began to confuse her and she quickly lost interest and began to talk loudly to her neighbor. Eventually Ruby's teacher sent her out of the circle because she was not quieting down, and Ruby lost even more time learning language.

All children's brains develop based on the stimulation and experiences they have. For children who have experienced trauma, this can lead to their coming into our classrooms with some regions of their brains significantly underdeveloped, such as Ruby's language development, while other areas that are overused are overdeveloped and stronger than what is typical (Child Welfare Information Gateway 2015). For example, while Ruby's language is behind her peers', she has very high nonverbal skills and watches her teacher and classmates closely, which she uses to navigate classroom situations when she does not understand the language being used.

Attachment and the Brain

Children's brains are profoundly shaped by the interactions between their genes and their experiences. While genes offer a blueprint for the construction of brain circuits, the circuits themselves are strengthened by their repeated use, which happens through children's earliest experiences. Thus the quality of the relationship between young children and their primary caregivers is a significant factor in young children's brain development. The attachment experience is a significant element of this developmental process; the "serve and return" interaction between babies and caregivers determines how babies see themselves and the world around them (National Scientific Council on the Developing Child 2012, 2015). This serve and return, or what developmental scholars and researchers call "contingent reciprocity," forms the connections that build the brain's architecture. Children learn to regulate their emotions and behaviors by expressing their wants and needs (the serve) and learning how their caregivers respond to them (the return). The ways in which their primary caregivers interact with them allows children to internalize and believe in the security of these relationships. The quality of the relationship creates children's internal working models, which informs how children see themselves and the world around them (Bowlby 1980; Newman, Sivaratnam, and Komiti 2015).

Research demonstrates that across cultures there are many ways to show nurturance and care for children, but the primary experience of feeling protected, heard, and understood helps children feel confident that they have adults who care for them (Barrett and Fleming 2011). They learn that if they do not know how to handle a difficult situation, they can find individuals who can support them in finding a solution. When babies cry, smile, babble, or laugh and their adult responds appropriately, they are learning that when they express their needs, good things happen to them, and their brains see the world as a safe and predictable place (Newman, Sivaratnam, and Komiti 2015). Significantly, what is considered "appropriate" varies across cultures but can include things such as eye contact, words, or facial expressions—all of which are affirming responses that allow for the building and strengthening of neural connections in children's brains. Healthy and attached relationships between caregivers and children can look different across cultural and racial groups. Healthy attachment is not as simple as responding to children in the "right" way; rather, it is context based and culturally relative for the individual family and their background.

No matter the cultural background, from birth babies are neurologically primed for interaction and communication with their primary caregivers. Infants participate in an array of signaling behaviors to initiate and maintain connections with their primary caregivers. These signals can include making eye contact, imitating caregivers' facial expressions, and expressing distress through crying and grunting to initiate responses from their adults. Typically when children participate in these signaling behaviors, caregivers are able to respond with sensitivity and attunement, which develops the healthy neural connections that will support the infants in their emotional regulation throughout their lives. In healthy attachment relationships between an infant and adult, the adult becomes an "external psychobiological regulator" of the infant's emotional and behavioral arousal (Schore 2003, 185). Caregivers' abilities to respond appropriately to babies' signals influences babies' brain architecture and their developmental trajectories across the domains (Newman, Sivaratnam and Komiti 2015).

Contemporary research indicates that babies are especially sensitive to the affective state of their caregivers and can both quickly and correctly signal and assess emotional states. Infants tend to copy the emotional states they see in their caregivers and prefer "happy" facial expressions over expressions of anger (Newman, Sivaratnam, and Komiti 2015). The "Still-Face" experiment, which was originally conducted in 1978, demonstrates that maternal engagement and responsiveness influences infants' emotional states and capacities to regulate. Mothers were instructed to play face-to-face with their infants for two minutes before becoming affectively unresponsive; in other words, creating a blank face and simply looking at their babies. The children were found to respond with extreme suspicion, eventually disengaging when they did not receive feedback from the person who was supposed to help regulate them (Mesman, van Ijzendoorn, and Bakermans-Kranenburg 2009). These responses signify the importance of interaction between infants and their caregivers in supporting infants' emotional regulation. When infants do not receive the positive feedback from their caregivers that they are biologically primed for, they have higher levels of relational stress and more negative emotional states. When primary caregivers are not able to facilitate the attachment system for their infants and be the external regulators they need, infants experience disruption to the neurological development of the specific brain regions that support self-regulation and the processing of emotions (Newman, Sivaratnam, and Komiti 2015).

Typically when infants experience distress or feel threatened, parents or other caregivers support them in reestablishing a sense of safety and control over their lives. However, children who experience early separation, trauma, or maltreatment at the hands of trusted adults may not have the necessary experience of healthy attachment as a guide to regulate their emotions (Head Start Bulletin 2009). Because brain development is "experience-dependent" (Schore 2003, 73), children who have experienced early disruptions and traumas can have changes in specific brain regions concerned with emotional regulation (Newman, Sivaratnam, and Komiti 2015). When children lack the support needed to see them through stressful situations, it arrests their ability to work through and integrate what happened. This leaves young children at risk of becoming overwhelmed by feelings of distress and unable to regulate their internal emotional and physical states, changing their brain chemistry.

Trauma and the Brain

Ezekiel is a nine-month-old baby who recently entered full-time child care. Eze-kiel's mom left his father after a particularly scary domestic violence incident, and she went from being a stay-at-home mom to working full-time. Ezekiel is having a hard time transitioning into child care. He screams and cries when his mom leaves in the morning and has long stretches of being inconsolable. He also gets upset and screams every time a man comes into the room. When Ezekiel does finally calm down, he will not look at his caregivers and only wants to be by him-self. Developmentally Ezekiel is behind; he is not very responsive when teachers engage with him and is not yet babbling.

✋ ✋ ✋ ✋ ✋ ✋

Our increasing understanding of the effects of trauma and attachment relation-ships on the developing brain has demonstrated some of the specific neurobi-ological repercussions of early adverse experiences. Children who have chaotic or scary home lives with abusive or nonresponsive caregivers may develop neu-ronal connections that cause them to remain hyperalert for danger, or certain regions of their brain may fail to fully develop. As is the case for Ezekiel, this can impact their behavior and relationships in the classroom. Ezekiel cannot be soothed by his teachers when upset and then wants to be alone once calm. This is because his early experience of trauma has already changed his neuro-nal pathways and made him hyperalert to possible danger. Ezekiel is constantly scanning his environment for danger and worries that any man entering his classroom may become a source of danger. His fear of men is causing his body to respond with big feelings, hindering his ability to respond to his teachers' love and nurturance—and making it difficult for them to connect to him and to help him feel safe.

The ways in which trauma influences brain development depends on mul-tiple factors. The age of a child at the time of the trauma, the type and severity of the trauma, whether the trauma was acute or complex, the role of the abuser in the child's life, whether the child has at least one healthy attachment figure, and other individual and environmental factors affect how the child processes the experience (Child Welfare Information Gateway 2015; van der Kolk 2014).

As noted earlier, both gene expression and environmental experience play a fundamental role in brain development, and the disruption of either can change the brain's architecture. Not only are early experiences crucial for brain development, but "sensitive periods" also allow for optimal brain growth and development. These periods are the times when certain parts of the brain are most easily affected by experiences in both positive and negative ways. During a sensitive developmental window, the brain is most likely to be open to the development of specific milestones. As the sensitive period ends, the neural circuits organize and stabilize, which leads to consistency in behavioral response. Conversely, atypical experiences during a sensitive period can lead to developmental abnormalities within the brain (Hartley and Lee 2014).

Studying these periods of sensitivity is difficult because of the necessity for ethical considerations in research. However, what we do know is that synapses and neuronal pathways must be consistently activated to ensure that they are not erroneously pruned. For example, infants are wired to form attachments to their primary caregivers, and if offered healthy one-on-one contact, babies will create strong, trusting, and durable bonds to the adults closest to them. However, in situations where infants are severely neglected and not offered consistent caregiving, babies can end up losing some of their ability to form healthy attachments and bonds, even if offered a loving and stable home later in life (van der Kolk 2014).

Effects of Trauma on the Brain

While brain research is a developing field and we are learning more all the time about the impact of trauma on the brain, we know that specific regions of the brain and hormones that can potentially be affected by trauma can in turn influence children's needs in the classroom. Research indicates that changes can occur in the following regions of the brain.

Amygdala. The amygdala responds to fear, threat, and danger and plays an important role in emotional regulation and perceiving emotions in others (Thomason and Marusak 2017). The amygdala is essential to survival because it helps us assess imminent danger and react almost instantaneously. For all children, the amygdala helps quickly determine if something is a threat based on past experiences with similar sounds or images. For example, think back to the mama crocodile in chapter 1. You are walking down by the water and suddenly see shapes that look like a mama crocodile and her hatchlings. The incoming information takes a short route from the thalamus to the amygdala, which allows your brain to set into motion the physiological response to quickly fight, flee, or freeze from this perceived threat to help you survive. However, this time what you are seeing is actually not a crocodile; it is a fallen tree trunk and branches that look like a crocodile and her hatchlings. At the same time as your amygdala has started to respond, the shape you see will pass through the thalamus on to the cortex, which will realize a fraction of a second later that the shapes you thought were a mama crocodile and her hatchlings are actually parts of a fallen tree. At this point, your heart stops racing and you will realize you had a momentary scare but there's no ongoing threat. However, for children who have experienced trauma, the amygdala is overstimulated to the point that it can become overwhelmed by the amount of information it needs to process. This can lead to two different changes. First, as with Ezekiel, the amygdala can become overactive and remain on high alert, resulting in a child who is anxious, fearful, and hypervigilant. The child may be in fight-or-flight mode in the classroom even when there is no external threat. Second, an overwhelmed amygdala can shut down as a way of protecting the child from the feeling of being in danger. This child will freeze or dissociate as a protective measure even when there is no threat present (National Scientific Council on the Developing Child 2010b). This can lead to children shutting down in the classroom and missing out on the important experiences of play and early learning they need.

Hippocampus. The hippocampus is the region of the brain that processes emotions and memories and is essential for both long-term memory storage and learning. Trauma can impede the hippocampus's ability to store and recall memories in sequential order (National Scientific Council on the Developing Child 2014). This can lead to children in the classroom not being able to follow multistep directions and needing extra support to memorize and learn basic skills.

Corpus callosum. Children who have experienced maltreatment often have a reduced volume in the corpus callosum, which connects the left and right sides of the brain. This can lead to less integration of the two halves of the brain. When the two sides of a child's brain cannot integrate effectively, communication between brain regions can be inhibited, which can lead to an increase in behavioral issues and dissociative symptoms (Teicher et al. 2016).

Cerebellum. Research has consistently shown decreased cerebellar volume in children who have experienced maltreatment. The cerebellum is primarily known for its part in coordinating motor development. However, it also plays a role in processing emotions, fear conditioning, and cognition, all of which can be impaired in children who have experienced trauma (McCrory, De Brito, and Viding 2010).

Prefrontal cortex. The prefrontal cortex plays an important role in executive function, which is the higher-level cognition that allows an individual to differentiate between opposing ideas, understand good and bad, and connect current actions with future outcomes. Children who experience toxic stress can have less-efficient prefrontal cortex activity; living in chaotic or neglectful environments can make it difficult for young children to access and engage their executive abilities, even when they are in safe situations. This can lead to children who have experienced trauma having difficulty in the classroom with long-term thinking, understanding cause and effect, and staying regulated and calm (National Scientific Council on the Developing Child 2011; Teicher et al. 2016).

Attachment, the Brain, and Memory Formation

Young children who have experienced trauma may not be able to *recall* their earliest traumatic experiences, but their bodies do *remember* them. And the ways in which their bodies remember the experiences shape the way young children see themselves and the world. Through healthy attachment relationships, children learn that when they smile, they usually receive a smile in return; when they have feelings, they are typically attended to; and when they venture out on their own, they will have someone to return to. After having these experiences repeatedly, children's brains begin to manage these experiences easily because memories have been formed, which facilitates easy and quick information sharing between brain regions. Creating memories is vitally important for children's well-being; it is through these memories that they create beliefs about the world and form the skills they need for survival and growth. However, for young children who have experienced trauma, their earliest experiences can negatively impact the way they see the world (National Scientific Council on the Developing Child 2010a, 2014).

Newborns have the ability to form implicit memories, which are the memories that are remembered unconsciously but greatly affect thoughts and behaviors. Babies' early implicit memories, formed through their earliest attachment relationships, may shape their views on subsequent relationships. If their care-givers at home are unpredictable or scary, they will expect similar treatment from teachers and school personnel as well.

Unlike implicit memories, explicit memories are conscious memories that individuals can recall. Explicit memories typically begin to occur around two years old and allow children to talk about things that happened in the past and things that will happen in the future. For instance, a two-year-old may say, "Remember painting?" to initiate a conversation about what they did that morning. Or when you announce that it's naptime, they may say, "No, I go to the park!" to share what they would like to do instead. Children who have experienced trauma may not be able to access explicit memories about their traumatic experiences because they are not able to organize those experiences in sequential order, though they may have implicit memories of the physical or emotional sensations that occurred while they experienced the trauma. In the classroom, these implicit memories can cause flashbacks, nightmares, or quick reactions to specific noises, smells, or shapes that trigger a reminder of their traumatic experience. For example, a crawling six-month-old baby who has experienced domestic violence in her home may visibly lurch forward when her teacher gently redirects her away from a sleeping child. Even when the teacher uses a calm voice to quickly say, "Uh-oh, let's let Raquel sleep," a heightened baby may jump. While there is no immediate danger, the pace of the teacher's words as she tries to ensure the other baby can continue to sleep may trigger the infant and cause her to respond from her implicit memory of fear and anxiety.

Epigenetics

An emerging field of research, epigenetics, is offering more clues about ways in which intergenerational trauma and the external environment can change gene expression and function, which can then be heritable. Epigenetics refers to the chemical changes or "signatures" that can mark specific genes, influencing gene expression. These modifications can influence the expression of genes in brain cells permanently or temporarily and, significantly, can then be inherited by an individual's biological children (Isobel et al. 2018; National Scientific Council on the Developing Child 2010a). Genes receive cues from the environment and one's experiences, which influence their expression. Prenatal and early experiences, living situations, and the race- and class-based interactions a young child has are all factors that, in part, determine how genes respond (National Scientific Council on the Developing Child 2010a, 2010b). Importantly, parental care and comfort can influence gene expression, making the role of the adult greatly important for young children (Isobel et al. 2018). The Child Welfare Information Gateway (2015) explains:

> Although the field of epigenetics is still in its infancy, studies have indicated that child maltreatment can cause epigenetic modifications in victims. In one study of individuals with posttraumatic stress disorder (PTSD), those who had been maltreated as children exhibited more epigenetic changes in genes associated with central nervous system development and immune system regulation than nonmaltreated individuals with PTSD (Mehta et al. 2013). (7)

On the other hand, positive and supportive care as well as rich learning environments can create healthy epigenetic signatures that fuel genetic potential (National Scientific Council on the Developing Child 2010b).

Neuroplasticity

While brain development can be heavily influenced by children's earliest experiences, the brain also has an amazing ability to rewire, change, and reorganize in response to new experiences. This ability is called "neuroplasticity." Amazingly, just as young children's brains can change due to traumatic or stressful environments, they can also change when exposed to supportive environments (van der Kolk 2014). Although a child may experience adverse childhood experiences, brain plasticity can counteract some of the effects. The plasticity of children's brains is dependent on the region of the brain or brain system affected and the particular developmental stage of the individual children (Siegel and Payne Bryson 2011). The more primitive areas of the brain, such as the brainstem and midbrain, which control involuntary functions, are less malleable or plastic than higher-functioning areas of the brain, such as the limbic system and cortex (Child Welfare Information Gateway 2015).

While neuroplasticity is especially common in young children, which is why early childhood is such a critical period for appropriate trauma-responsive environments, some degree of plasticity remains throughout adolescence and adulthood, which is what allows learning into old age (van der Kolk 2014). Imagine brain development like the construction of a house. First the plans are drawn up, and then the foundation is laid. Next come the walls and windows, and finally the roof. Once construction is completed, you can walk through your new house and decide the kitchen windows were placed in the wrong spot and the dining room wall should be moved two feet to the north. With time and money, both of these things can be done, but it would have been easier and cheaper if the changes had been made before the whole house was built. Similarly, brain plasticity may allow children and adults to change their brains' architecture and recuperate from missed experiences, yet it is probable that making these changes later in life will be more difficult and possibly not as effective. This difficulty is even more pronounced for children who did not experience much stimulation to specific brain regions, which leads to the discarding of neuronal connections. Thus children who do not have a strong foundational network of neuronal pathways to support their brains' optimal functioning may have a harder time learning and mastering future developmental goals, which is why we must make sure all early learning environments are trauma responsive (Child Welfare Information Gateway 2015).

Conclusion

Brain development and children's earliest experiences are intertwined in significant ways. Children who have experienced trauma are likely to have changes in their brains that influence how they see and interact with the world around them. Children's learning and experiences in school settings must be responsive to their earliest experiences at home to effectively support and reach all learners. Neuroplasticity demonstrates that children's emotions, behaviors, and cognitive understanding can change based on healthy and reparative interactions, which makes the role of the teacher and the school environment so deeply important. Our role as educators and school administrators is both to understand and offer different experiences for young children who have experienced trauma.

Chapter 3

Adverse Childhood Experiences, Resilience, and Protective Factors

Many children who experience early trauma or stressors do not experience lasting negative effects, while others go on to have significant consequences to their neurodevelopmental and immune systems. While certain stressors put children at a higher risk for negative mental and behavioral outcomes, these stressors may affect children differently depending on the individual differences between children, a child's age when the exposure to the adverse experience occurs, and whether the experience was an isolated incident or occurred in conjunction with other risk factors. This chapter highlights the effects of early trauma on children's schooling and adult lives as well as the positive impact resilience and protective factors, such as responsive schools and educators, can have on young children.

Consider for a moment Amari, an eight-year-old who was adopted by his great-aunt and great-uncle at eighteen months. Amari's mom was a teenager in foster care when he was born. She herself had experienced significant trauma and mental health issues as well as substance abuse issues. Amari was born with neonatal abstinence syndrome (NAS) and spent three weeks in the neonatal intensive care unit before being separated from his mother and placed in foster care. At four months, he was reunited with his mother in a drug and alcohol rehabilitation facility where she had been sober for one and a half months. After six months with his mom, it was discovered that she had relapsed, and Amari was sent to a foster home. Over the next nine months, he moved through two more foster homes, all the while having inconsistent weekly visits with his mom. At eighteen months, he was moved across the country to his adoptive home, at which point his visits with his mom ended. All of his foster homes described him as an "easy baby"; he ate well, slept well, loved to engage with people, and had a soft cry that was easy for his caregivers to respond to. His parents describe him similarly; he was a content toddler and always independent, wanting to do things for himself. He never had many concerning big behaviors. They delighted in his easygoing temperament right away and said they often "forgot" he did not join their family until he was a toddler.

Amari is now eight and in third grade. His two-year-old biological brother recently moved into his home also to be adopted. Amari is smart, loving, funny, and well liked by his peers, but his behaviors have recently escalated at home and at school. Amari is having a difficult time regulating his emotions at school. He is physical with his peers, pushing or yelling to get what he wants, and has recently gone from being extremely independent to being overly focused on vying for affection and attention from his teacher. If he feels like there is competition for his teacher's time, he often disrupts the classroom until attention, positive or negative, is inevitably turned to him.

Amari's family describes these new behaviors as "coming out of nowhere"; however, he is one of thousands of children we see in our schools every day who have experienced early trauma. His younger brother's addition to his family has pushed Amari beyond his capacity to cope with his feelings of loss and abandonment, which stem from his multiple early attachment disruptions. Deep down Amari has never felt worthy of the love and nurturance he wants and needs. Even as a toddler, he tried to protect himself from getting too attached by always being independent and capable of caring for himself. Now, having to split the attention in his home with his younger brother, he is constantly worried that he is not good enough and his parents will stop loving him.

These worries and concerns are causing him to act out in ways that are surprising to everyone in his life, including Amari. To best support Amari in the classroom, the impact of Amari's early experiences must be understood. Early adversity influences young children like Amari differently depending on several factors, including the frequency and number of traumas experienced as well as the risk factors and protective factors that can amplify or buffer traumatic events.

The Adverse Childhood Experiences Study

Between 1995 and 1997, Dr. Robert Anda and Dr. Vincent Felitti spearheaded a landmark two-wave study between Kaiser Permanente and the Centers for Disease Control to examine the relationship between adverse childhood experiences (ACEs—stressful or traumatic events in childhood), and their subsequent impact on mental and physical health in adulthood (Felitti et al. 1998).

This groundbreaking study, which included more than seventeen thousand adults who were insured through Kaiser Permanente, showed that ACEs were far more widespread than formerly believed and strongly correlated with negative health outcomes in adulthood. This was one of the primary studies that led researchers and scholars to notice and respond to early childhood trauma as a meaningful and impactful public health issue that required attention and focus. Finally, there was concrete evidence that children did not simply forget their early trauma; rather, it stayed with them and affected their life trajectories.

The study asked participants to disclose whether they had experienced any of the following ten adverse experiences as children:

- physical abuse

- emotional abuse

- sexual abuse

- physical neglect

- emotional neglect

- substance abuse in the home

- a mentally ill or suicidal household member

- mother treated violently

- parental separation or divorce

- parental incarceration

While there are many other traumatic life experiences that can have lasting adverse effects (such as war, long hospital stays, homelessness, a pandemic, and so forth), this study focused on these ten ACEs, and these ten adversities alone produced staggering results. The researchers found that ACEs are extremely common, with more than one quarter of the individuals (28 percent) reporting they experienced physical abuse, 21 percent reporting they had experienced sexual abuse, 15 percent reporting they had experienced emotional neglect, and 10 percent reporting they had experienced physical neglect (Felitti et al. 1998).

Thinking back to Amari, he had experienced several ACEs before the age of eighteen months: emotional neglect, substance abuse and mental illness in the home, and separation from his parent and subsequent caregivers. Like Amari's experience, the study found that ACEs are vastly more prevalent than previously thought; over half of all participants had experienced at least one ACE, approximately 25 percent of the subjects had experienced two or more ACEs, and one out of sixteen participants experienced four or more ACEs as children. Most importantly, the study found that there is a clear "dose response" to ACEs, meaning that the more ACEs one experiences as a child, the higher the likelihood they will have physical or mental health issues as an adult (Felitti et al. 1998, 251). Adverse childhood experiences are one of the most powerful predictors of health, not only because they are a driving force behind many different health and health-risk issues, but also because they account for such a large percentage of each of these issues. For example, childhood traumas are predictive of the following:

- early introduction to alcohol use and continued problem drinking into adulthood

- early introduction to tobacco use and continued tobacco use throughout adulthood

- prescription and illicit drug use and misuse

- depression

- sleep disturbances

- suicidal thoughts and behaviors

- anxiety disorders

In addition, this study found that the more ACEs experienced, the more likely one was to develop physical health issues such as the following:

- liver disease

- cancer

- diabetes

- stroke

- heart disease

This study allowed social scientists and practitioners working with children and adults to begin to understand the prevalence and impact of trauma on physical and mental health issues. Children who experience trauma are more likely to participate in health-risk behaviors and experience resulting health problems that influence their well-being into adulthood, up to and including early death (Felitti et al. 1998).

It is important to note that the participants in the ACE study were primarily white, middle class, and college educated, so they do not represent the true demographics of the entire US population, but the study did give the beginning information needed to expand research on the impact of trauma across one's lifespan. Further, it helped dispel the myth that trauma only happens to those experiencing poverty. While it is true that poverty increases the likelihood a child will be exposed to ACEs due to the reasons for and stressors of living in poverty, poverty alone is not an adverse childhood experience (Burke Harris 2018; Vanderbilt-Adriance and Shaw 2008). Children from all socioeconomic, cultural, religious, and familial backgrounds can have adverse childhood experiences.

Adverse Childhood Experiences and School

While the ACE study offered us a clear and profound link between early experiences of trauma and later health issues, it did not expound on the immediate effects trauma can have on children themselves. However, since the initial ACE study, research has looked at the developmental effects trauma exposure has on children, and it has now been demonstrated that trauma profoundly influences development and children's learning (Burke Harris 2018; van der Kolk 2014). For example, a 2014 study of three- to four-year-old children attending federally funded Head Start programs found that children's ACE exposure was associated with lower teacher ratings of social-emotional and cognitive development (Blodgett 2014). Teachers rated children who had experienced ACEs lower on the following developmental domains:

- social-emotional development

- literacy development

- language development

- cognitive development

- math development

In this study and others (Jimenez et al. 2016; Scott et al. 2013), ACEs were found to be predictors of developmental concerns in social-emotional skills as well as early academic domains connected to school readiness (Blodgett 2014).

The findings that ACEs increase academic challenges hold true for the elementary years as well. ACEs have a powerful effect on elementary students' engagement in school and academic competence. A 2011 study looking at the effects of ACEs on 2,101 students ages five to eleven years old (grades K–6) found that 44 percent of the students experienced one or more ACE, and 13 percent of students experienced three or more ACEs. This study found that even exposure to one ACE increases the likelihood of poor outcomes for a student. Further, just as ACEs have a dose response for adults, this is true for students as well: the more ACEs experienced, the more likely it is there will be developmental repercussions for students. For example, compared to their peers with zero ACEs, a student with one adverse childhood experience was 1.6 times more likely to have academic concerns at school; a student with two adverse childhood experiences was 2.5 times more likely to have academic concerns; a student with three adverse childhood experiences was 3.1 times more likely to have academic concerns, and a student with four or more adverse childhood experiences was 3.4 times as likely to have academic concerns. Their findings went beyond academic challenges and demonstrated that students who experienced ACEs were also more likely to struggle with behavior and attendance as well (Blodgett and Lanigan 2018). Figure 3.1 describes the findings of this study.

Figure 3.1. The Connection between ACEs Experienced and School and Physical Health

	Academic Concerns	Behavioral Concerns	Attendance Concerns
Zero ACEs	1.0	1.0	1.0
1 ACE	1.6	2.4	2.0
2 ACEs	2.5	4.8	2.7
3 ACEs	3.1	4.8	4.5
4+ ACEs	3.4	6.9	4.9

The more ACEs a child experiences, the greater likelihood of school-related concerns.

While it is clear that trauma can cause lasting damage and effects on the developing child, research also shows us that not everyone responds to trauma in the same way. For some, traumatic experiences can occur without arresting their development or overwhelming their bodies and brains (Felitti et al. 1998). As Resnick and Taliaferro (2012) describe, "Clearly, the piling on of risk factors increases the vulnerability of individuals or systems to poor outcomes, but thresholds vary as to 'how much is too much' in terms of experiencing damage or harm" (300). Therefore although the presence of risk factors typically increases the likelihood of experiencing the results of trauma, it does not necessarily mean children will experience the negative outcomes trauma can cause. Despite experiencing risk factors, protective factors can have a profound influence on children's development (Moore 2013).

Resilience and Protective Factors

Carley is eight years old and currently in second grade. Born with a heart condition, she went into heart failure at four and spent several months in the hospital waiting for a heart transplant. She was able to get a heart transplant, but she was in and out of the hospital until she was five and a half. Because of this, she started kindergarten at six. She has been healthy and thriving for three years now, and if you did not know her story, you would never guess that Carley spent nearly a year living in a hospital. Carley's extended family and church community rallied around her and her parents, offering meals, rides, and housecleaning support. Further, Carley's parents' flexible schedules allowed one of them to be with her at all times in the hospital so she was never alone. Carley's parents spent a lot of time reading to her in the hospital and playing games. Carley had to start school a year late due to being in the hospital for most of what should have been her kindergarten year, yet she has had no academic or social problems at school.

Although there is increased evidence that early childhood stressors and disrupted attachment can lead to changes in the brain and resulting behavioral changes, not all children who experience risk factors experience negative neural consequences. *Resilience* can be defined as the ability to maintain or return to healthy functioning when adversity occurs. If an individual lacks resiliency, a challenge or stressor may overwhelm their capacity to cope and move through the difficult experience. Resilience does not make the problems go away, but it can help an individual see beyond the current moment and still find pleasure in life (Child Welfare Information Gateway 2014b; National Scientific Council on the Developing Child 2015).

Resilient adaptation is not a skill that children either have or do not have; rather, it is the response to the interaction between their personal experiences and the protective social factors in their environment. Take Carley, for example. Although Carley experienced a complex trauma, living in the hospital for nearly a year, she was shielded from many of the negative effects of the trauma by having a strong support system of family and church community surrounding her and her parents throughout the entire ordeal. Carley entered kindergarten feeling confident and capable because she had always been supported by her family at home, and she expected her teacher to do the same. Experiencing stressors can have a great impact on young children's mental health, or it can have little or no impact, depending on individual differences between children, their age when the stressor occurs, and whether the stressor is coupled with other risk factors or happens alone (National Scientific Council on the Developing Child 2015; Plumb, Bush, and Kersevich 2016).

Resilience results from a combination of protective factors. Protective factors are the characteristics of the individual child, their family, and their wider community or environment that reduce the damaging effects of adversity on the child's developmental, academic, and health outcomes. Protective factors can essentially be divided into two camps: disposition and luck (Child Welfare Information Gateway 2014b; Plumb, Bush, and Kersevich 2016).

Children's development is continuously influenced by the negative and positive experiences they have throughout their childhoods. As Shonkoff and Phillips (2000) explain, "Individual developmental pathways throughout the life cycle are influenced by interactions among risk factors that increase the probability of a poor outcome and protective factors that increase the probability of a positive outcome" (30). Risk factors can be both personal (for example, a difficult temperament or physical abnormalities) and environmental (for example, physical abuse or poverty). Similarly, protective factors can be both personal (for example, a pleasant temperament or above-average intelligence) and environmental (for example, a healthy attachment to a primary caregiver or supportive community). Research demonstrates that risk factors are cumulative;

the more children have, the higher their likelihood of developmental repercussions. And in reverse, the more protective factors children have, the higher their likelihood of developmental resilience (van der Kolk 2014; Plumb, Bush, and Kersevich 2016).

The power and effect of resiliency bring to light the importance of seeing children's individual strengths as well as seeing them within the context of their families and communities. Rather than seeing individual deficits or disorders, research on resiliency allows us to recognize the strengths and protective factors that support young children in overcoming the adversity they experience (Child Welfare Information Gateway 2014b). As trauma-responsive educators and administrators, we can build on children's strengths and protective factors to help them navigate and find success in our classrooms and schools.

Children are less likely to experience the adverse effects of stress and trauma if they believe they are worthy of good things. This sense of worthiness in young children is more likely to occur for those who have strong familial attachments and relationships within their communities. Certain characteristics, such as high intelligence, an appealing appearance, and an easy, flexible, and social temperament have been shown to increase connection between children and adults. These factors influence how children see the world and how adults in schools see and respond to children; children who are cute and easygoing are much more likely to get positive attention from both children and adults, which allows them to build a positive identity. These protective factors allow children to develop deep connections with the adults in their lives and have a sense of achievement and accomplishment across their environments (home, school, and community).

To get a well-rounded understanding of protective factors and their effect, I will highlight a few of the most well-researched protective factors.

Temperament. Having an easygoing and social personality is a protective factor for young children. Some children are calm and easy to be around from birth, while other children are more emotionally reactive, which can make it harder for adult caregivers to stay calm and find joy in them from infancy and beyond (SAMHSA 2012). Having an easy temperament or personality allows children to navigate and overcome adversity. This is one of the protective factors that supported Amari, the eight-year-old introduced in the beginning of this chapter, in doing as well as he has. Amari was an easygoing and joyful baby, which allowed each of his caregivers to connect with him and delight in him, even during his short stays in their homes. Having an easy temperament has also allowed Amari to build strong relationships with his classmates and teachers; everyone has always enjoyed his company.

High intelligence. The benefit of high intelligence has been widely researched and validated. Children with higher-than-average intelligence often have a greater capacity to process information and problem solve, which allows them to proactively deal with the stressors and challenges they experience. Further, high intelligence can allow children to excel academically, making them feel like a part of our learning communities and offering them the skills to recognize and conform to social norms, which furthers their connection to both their peers and adults. While above-average or high intelligence is not the only protective factor, it is a prominent and relatively stable factor that influences children's resiliency (Vanderbilt-Adriance and Shaw 2008).

Age. Stressors affect children differently depending on the age when exposure occurs. Older children tend to do better with adverse experiences than young children because the basic foundations of their brains are more developed. Older children have their healthy early experiences to ground their understanding of themselves and the world around them when adversity—such as neglect, witnessing or experiencing violence, or having caregivers experiencing substance abuse—strikes (SAMHSA 2012).

Healthy attachment. As discussed in chapter 2, healthy attachment is one of the primary protective factors for children. Consistent nurturing and responsive parenting strategies are connected to low externalizing and internalizing behaviors. Through healthy early relationships at home and in the classroom, children learn to regulate their emotions as well as connect to the people around them. Like Carley, whose attachment relationships were never disrupted, children who have experienced early healthy attachment are more likely to be able to follow directions, listen to peers and teachers, and demonstrate prosocial behavior in school (Child Welfare Information Gateway 2014b). In his groundbreaking book *The Body Keeps the Score*, Bessel van der Kolk (2014) discusses the seminal work of Alan Sroufe, who studied how relationships shape child development. Van der Kolk describes to the reader how Sroufe "learned a great deal about resilience: the capacity to bounce back from adversity. By far the most important predictor of how well his subjects coped with life's inevitable disappointments was the level of security established with their primary care-giver during the first two years of life. Sroufe informally told me that he thought that resilience in adulthood could be predicted by how lovable mothers rated their kids at age two" (161). Early healthy attachment sets children up for a life-time of healthy, prosocial relationships.

Family stability. Consistent employment, financial stability, and housing stability are all protective factors for children. When families are stable, there is less adult stress, which allows for healthier relationships between the adults in the home as well as healthier attachment to children and more consistent par-enting strategies. All of these factors can help create the consistent and stable environments children need to thrive (Child Welfare Information Gateway 2014b; National Scientific Council on the Developing Child 2015).

Strong cultural identity. Connection to one's culture and community is protective for many children. For Amari, remaining within his biological family allowed him to continue to feel connected to his biological roots and supported in his identity development. Culture offers children a set of values, beliefs, tra-ditions, and behavioral norms that can support them in feeling like they are an active member of a community and give them a sense of belonging that allows them to see themselves as a part of something concrete and special (National Scientific Council on the Developing Child 2015).

Involvement with a faith or religious community. Faith and religious communities often offer children environments of safety, love, and com-munal norms. They allow children to build healthy relationships and a value system that is predictable and consistent. The research demonstrates that being involved in a faith-based community works as a protective factor for children who experience early trauma or stress (Child Welfare Information Gateway 2014b; National Scientific Council on the Developing Child 2015). The support Carley's family received from their church and her continued participation in her church's youth programming allows her to feel connected to a community larger than her own family.

Figure 3.2 outlines an extensive list of the many risk and protective factors that can influence young children's development.

Figure 3.2.

Risk Factors/ Threats to Resiliency	Domain	Protective Factors
• Difficult temperament: being inflexible, poor concentration, withdrawing behavior, and low mood. • Mental health issues: low self-esteem, anxiety, depressive symptoms • Attachment difficulties • Lacking social skills: low capacity for effective communication and problem solving • High need for external approval and support • Shyness • Emotional dysregulation • Behavioral challenges	Individual	• Above-average/high intelligence • Academic achievement/ capacity • High self-esteem • Emotional regulation skills • Social skills: effective coping skills and problem-solving skills • Engagement and connections with school, peers, athletics, religion, or culture
• Mental health issues in the household: depression, anxiety, suicidal thoughts or behaviors, schizophrenia, and more • Family conflict: conflict between the adults, the adults and children, and between children • Inadequate parenting and supervision • Family member substance abuse • Housing instability • Child abuse and neglect • Divorce • Parent/caregiver unemployment	Family	• Family is predictable, has clear and appropriate boundaries and rules • Family members are supportive and caring • Family values are upheld

	Community/ Environment	
• Rejection by peers and adults • Living in a high-crime area • Community- or school-based traumatic or violent incidents • Failing school • Losing close relationships or friends		• Faith-based community • Sense of cultural belonging • Presence of supportive community • Healthy school culture • Clear and high expectations for behavior within school and community • Physical and psychological safety

Building Resilience

Historically child abuse prevention has focused on lessening risk factors; however, practitioners now believe that building protective factors and one's capacity for resilience is another great way to mitigate the negative effects of trauma (Child Welfare Information Gateway 2014b; SAMHSA 2012). As trauma-responsive educators and administrators, we can focus on children's strengths and support them in building their capacities. Therefore, although a child may experience several risk factors, early childhood schools and classrooms that are trauma responsive can offer new and different experiences to counteract the effects of risk factors on the brain. Because we know that the brains of children under the age of seven have a high degree of plasticity, it is critical that we build young children's resilience in the early years.

To reduce or mitigate the impact of ACEs and risk factors on young children's development, trauma-responsive teachers and schools can offer what Seibel and colleagues (2006) describe as the five Rs:

Relationships that offer safety, security, and love. Relationships built from care ensure that children feel worthy of good things happening to them.

Responsive interactions that ensure children see they can have a positive impact on the world. When a child initiates a sound, activity, or conversation and gets an affirming response from an adult, the child is learning—just as newborns are primed to learn—that who they are and what they do matters in the world.

Respect for children and their families. To understand who each individual child is in a holistic manner, it is imperative that we understand their family, culture, and identity. By seeing and responding to a child as a full person worthy of respect and rights, teachers can demonstrate that who that child is matters, supporting the child in building their self-esteem.

Routines offer predictability to children, and for children who have experienced trauma, this may be the first time they have experienced any sort of consistency. Having an anticipated rhythm every day supports children's memory development, supports early organizational skills, and can lessen hypervigilance.

Repetition, repetition, and more repetition allows children's brains to make connections and strengthen connections between brain cells. For many children who have experienced trauma, this repetition allows them to build capacity for activities and ways of being that they have never experienced before.

Conclusion

Amari's story teaches us that both risk factors and protective factors can influence how well children do at home and school. Without a trauma-responsive lens, Amari's emerging difficulties in third grade could be overlooked as simply behavioral rather than as a manifestation of his overwhelming feelings and inability to cope with the many ACEs he experienced before the age of two. Through Carley we are also able to see that with strong attachment relationships and warm community supports, not all children who experience trauma will have trauma symptoms and negative repercussions as a result of the adversity in their stories.

Chapter 4

Expression of Trauma in the Classroom

Cognitive Development

_____

To HELP EXPLAIN HOW EARLY TRAUMA can influence development and academic learning, I am going to introduce you to two different children in the same first-grade classroom: Susan and Jennifer.

Susan: Susan is the second child of two loving and responsive parents. Her parents were married for eight years before she was born, and she is the light of their lives. Her family has experienced a few minor disruptions: they moved to a new house when Susan was two years old, and her dog died when she was six. However, with each of these experiences, her parents allowed her to express her feelings and helped her process them, so she did not feel confused or alone. Susan was lucky to find a child her own age on her block, Jennifer, and they have been best friends since they met at two. They have had a strong friendship and spend long afternoons playing together. Susan has always loved school and attended a small play-based preschool program that focused on supporting children's social-emotional development before starting kindergarten. She greatly enjoyed kindergarten and is enjoying first grade as well. She has a good group of friends and is excited to be able to read and write. She has loved her teachers and believes her teachers have loved her too.

Jennifer: Jennifer is Susan's best friend. They live on the same block. Just two houses separate them, but Jennifer feels like they live worlds apart. While Jennifer's home has been stable, everything else in her life has been chaotic. Jennifer's mom found out she was pregnant with Jennifer just as she had been working up the courage to leave her husband, who is both emotionally abusive and has an unhealthy relationship with alcohol. Once she found out she was pregnant with her first child, Jennifer's mom decided to stay for the sake of the baby. Jennifer's early years were filled with inconsistent caregiving: her mother loved her but could not emotionally handle caring for a baby and dealing with the emotional abuse from her husband. Jennifer's mom turned to alcohol to cope with her stress and unhappiness, and when Jennifer was little, her mother would drink to the point of becoming unresponsive on the couch as Jennifer played, leaving Jennifer to care for herself until her dad returned from work, when the fighting would begin. Jennifer learned to escape the chaos of her house by becoming good friends with her neighbor Susan. By the time Jennifer and Susan were in kindergarten, they spent every afternoon together, and that was the calmest time in Jennifer's life. At school Jennifer struggles. She cannot read and struggles with basic math concepts; falling behind academically has started to hurt her self-esteem. She has begun calling herself stupid, and when she cannot understand an assignment in class, she hits herself in the head or ends up acting out until she is sent out of the classroom. Her kindergarten teacher was happy to send her along to first grade at the end of the year because her behavior had been challenging and had not improved throughout her kindergarten year. Her current first-grade teacher also finds her very challenging and gets angry that Jennifer does not listen to her rules the way other students do. In anger and frustration, she ends up sending Jennifer to the principal's office multiple times a week.

Susan and Jennifer are two children who are both worthy of love and care. They both love playing with baby dolls, pretending to be teachers to their stuffed animals, and playing dress-up games. They both hold great strengths. One primary thing separates Susan and Jennifer from each other: trauma. Susan has experienced minimal trauma and disruption in her life, and Jennifer has experienced an overwhelming amount of trauma with few consistent supports in her life to help her cope with all that she has experienced. These two children have lived mere houses from each other for most of their lives, and yet they are having two drastically different experiences at home and school.

Although Susan and Jennifer love each other and find common ground in their play, the differences in their development and behavior are becoming more noticeable with each passing day. Jennifer's early trauma has disrupted her expected development, while Susan's consistent and loving home life has allowed her to flourish. These dear friends have vastly different capacities to attend to the tasks expected of them in the classroom. To expect Jennifer to respond to the academic and social aspects of the classroom similarly to Susan would inevitably cause more struggles and disappointment for both Jennifer and her teacher. Jennifer would be constantly disappointed in herself, and

Jennifer's teacher would be setting expectations that could not be met. To support and reach Jennifer, her teacher must first understand how trauma can disrupt development and then draw on Jennifer's strengths to build her skills and capacity to do well in the classroom.

Building off the research on brain development and attachment outlined in chapter 2, this chapter outlines some of the most common cognitive challenges children who have experienced trauma express in the classroom so that we can learn how to identify symptoms of trauma. Next, I discuss how cognition affects behavior and offer some concrete strategies teachers can use to support cognitive skills.

The Effect of Trauma on Cognitive Development

> Cognitive development: the ways children think, learn, process, reason, and abstract.

Experiencing trauma in early childhood can have long-term effects on children's cognitive development. Current research shows that children's views of the world begin to take shape in infancy, which influences how they see and interact with the world. This internal working model influences the development of the cognitive building blocks that affect future cognitive development. It has been shown that neglectful and abusive environments can slow cognitive functioning by late infancy, which can lead to lowered cognitive capacities for children who have experienced trauma in comparison to their peers (Cook et al. 2003; D'Andrea et al. 2012). Children who experience overwhelming stress can struggle with memory, problem solving, reasoning, and thinking through concepts. They may have trouble learning new skills or taking in new information. They can also have difficulties focusing and showing curiosity. Cognitive deficits in the early years can result in lower levels of academic achievement and higher rates of referral to special education than their nontraumatized peers (Cook et al. 2003; Blodgett and Lanigan 2018).

Trauma-responsive educators must be able to recognize delayed or missing cognitive milestones and find ways to adapt their teaching and classroom to support the children in achieving these milestones. To effectively assess and support each child's cognitive goals, teachers must have a strong understanding of child development and the ways that culture and community shape developmental norms.

For children who have experienced trauma, much of their internal energy may be spent focused on survival, constantly scanning the environment for safety threats. Continuously experiencing the stress response forces bodies and minds to constantly race, leaving little time to practice important cognitive skills. Children surviving in their emotional brains can find it difficult to engage their prefrontal cortices, which support children in the process of planning ahead, anticipating events in the future, and carrying out plans. These are all important executive functioning skills and very important for both academic and social success. Because of the time these children spend focused on survival, children who have been maltreated can have lower executive functioning skills compared to their non-maltreated peers, even in emotionally neutral contexts (D'Andrea et al. 2012).

Because children who have lived through maltreatment may not have the capacity to focus on their critical-thinking and cognitive skills, they may fall behind academically. Often they fall behind their peers cognitively in preschool, but the academic issues are not truly recognized until elementary school. Recognizing the widening gap between themselves and their peers can make school something they have negative feelings about; they may feel like their peers and teachers are reminders that they are not smart or capable. Let's take Jennifer, for example. Jennifer is struggling academically and is having a hard time memorizing the early literacy and math concepts she is expected to know. Jennifer's early life has caused her brain to develop differently than her friend Susan's. What seem like simple and straightforward tasks for Susan are challenging and often overwhelming tasks for Jennifer. Jennifer has a hard time concentrating, and she can see that school is becoming more challenging as the year progresses. She cannot understand why she is unable to complete the tasks that seem so simple for Susan, so she is starting to work on the hypothesis that it must be that she is just not smart. Jennifer needs a teacher who can support her in building new neural connections that allow her to see the classroom environment as a safe and connected space so that she can begin to feel calm enough to allow her brain to start to move toward higher-level thinking.

Sequencing and Cause and Effect

When cognitive development is interrupted by an inconsistent and unpredictable environment, children may find it challenging to understand sequencing, the cause-and-effect relationship, and their own capacity to affect what occurs around them (Plumb, Bush, and Kersevich 2016). Usually this cause-and-effect relationship occurs within the earliest attachment relationship. It's through relationship that children learn about their effect on the world and the relationship between different activities. As infants they learn that when they cry, someone comes for them. As they grow, they continue to learn about the cause-and-effect relationship. For example, when a one-year-old throws their food off their high chair over and over again, they are learning that every action has a reaction: *I drop my food on the ground, and my caregiver comes and picks it up.* This cause-and-effect relationship typically occurs during the first two years of life, as children are exploring their environment with their senses and motor development. As they explore, they learn that they can make things happen in the world around them. However, children who live with trauma may have their exploration restricted to the extent that they are unable to develop this cause-and-effect cognitive skill, or when they do explore, they get vastly different responses from their caregiver—for example, happy and affirming one day, angry and punitive the next. This prevents the child from learning consistency in response.

Not fully understanding the cause-and-effect relationship can lessen children's motivation to learn, impacting their behavior in the classroom environment. When children feel like they have a minimal impact on the world around them, it can hinder the development of capacities that are connected to having an impact on the world around them. For example, children may have a hard time setting goals for themselves, delaying gratification, or sequencing a set of tasks. These skills, which are paramount for academic success and a vital part of executive functioning, are dependent on children's abilities to see long-term goals. In the classroom, this may look like children who do not have goals for themselves: they may not be able to name subjects they want to learn or plan what career they'd like to have as adults, such as being a veterinarian or singer. Not only are these skills important for supporting academic success, but they are also very important for setting appropriate behavioral expectations as well; if children do not understand cause and effect, strategies that use traditional

behavior-management techniques and are dependent on punitive consequences will not be successful, and in fact they will probably be harmful.

Children who lack the support to make connections between their actions
and the responses they elicit may have concerns about the future since it can
seem both volatile and out of their control. Children living in chaotic environments may have a hard time trusting that the person who dropped them off at
school in the morning will be the same person who picks them up. When children experience their caregiver as loving one moment and angry or intoxicated
the next, they do not get a clear or consistent sense of who their caregiver is,
which can cause anxiety and fear every time they leave them. In the classroom,
this may look like children who have a very hard time separating from their
caregivers in the morning. They may cling to their adults and not want to enter
the classroom environment. At the end of the day, as other caregivers arrive,
they may start to display signs of anxiety and fear, running around the classroom without purpose, watching for their caregiver at the window, or exhibiting
behavior that is aggressive or volatile.

The Teacher's Role: Supporting Children's Understanding of Sequencing and Cause and Effect

Supporting children's cognitive development can take multiple forms and
involve multiple developmental domains. Susan wants to be a veterinarian
when she grows up; Jennifer cannot think of anything she wants to be. Jennifer
is having a hard time thinking of and planning for her future because she is so
focused on keeping herself safe in the present moment. Because sequencing
and planning can be difficult for children who have experienced trauma, we
need to implement strategies in the classroom that allow for practice of these
important skills. Here are a few ways we can support children in improving their
sequencing and planning skills:

- **Create a predictable environment.** Rhythm, routine, and ritual are
  ways to create predictability for young children so they know what
  to expect, which helps them feel calm. This frees up their mental
  energy to work on higher-level cognitive tasks like sequencing and
  future planning.

- **Do step-by-step projects.** Arts and crafts projects (such as using
  clay, tie-dyeing, or weaving) and baking projects or planning meals

allow children to follow directions and offer opportunities to plan into the not-so-distant future. Visual step-by-step instructions can be used to help children track the process and see the beginning to end product.

- **Use first/then images.** When children have difficulty remembering the order of events, teachers can make visual charts that state what happens first and what happens next, such as, "First we put on our shoes, and then we go outside." This can also happen in the moment using a small portable whiteboard. Simply draw what happens first and then what comes next.

- **Play.** Use play to build cognitive skills. Many forms of play involve planning and sequencing events. For example, in the dramatic play area, children need to decide which person will play each character and what those characters will do during play. At the art table, children have to figure out which material to use first (for example, sprinkle glitter or squeeze the glue first). In the building corner, children have to visualize what they are making and make decisions about which pieces will go where to make their structure work. Play can help children practice planning as well as following through on a task.

- **Use songs, games, and stories to practice sequencing.** Songs can be sung multiple times with small changes made so children must keep track of what has been said and what is coming. Games can be used to think about future planning, and stories can be created or cocreated by children to include beginnings, middles, and endings. These strategies allow children to use multisensory modes of practicing sequencing and planning.

- **Offer questions as support.** Trying to organize their thoughts or stories can overwhelm children. We can offer some phrases and questions to support them in organizing and sequencing their thoughts. Of course, it is always helpful to tailor our questions to the specific child and story they are telling, but here are a few sample sentences that can be used:

  - What happened first? Then what happened second? How did it end?

- Who was with you?

- Where were you?

- Were you inside or outside?

- Was it in the morning or after lunch?

- How long were you there?

- Were other people around?

Working Memory

As I discussed in chapter 2, early trauma can influence memory formation. *Working memory*, which allows children to process and recall information stored in the short-term memory, greatly influences cognitive functioning in the classroom. It is working memory that helps children move from being able to complete one-step directions to two- or three-step directions. For example, Jennifer's teacher asks each child to find their book for silent reading time and then meet over on the rug for a quick check-in before they begin reading. Jennifer's book is in her backpack, so she goes over to grab it, but by the time she has done that, she has forgotten the rest of the task she is supposed to complete; she does realize her backpack is dirty, however, and starts to gather the extra papers and bits of trash from inside to throw away. Jennifer's teacher finds her in the back of the classroom engrossed in this new activity with her book sitting unread by her side. Jennifer's behavior is not defiance. She is not trying to upset her teacher, although she does; she is simply having trouble with her working memory. From Jennifer's point of view, she is being really responsible by cleaning out her backpack. Trouble with working memory can cause challenges in several academic areas, including reading and math.

The Teacher's Role: Supporting Children's Working Memory

There are two primary ways to support working memory. First, we can offer working memory boosters—ways for children to practice their working memory skills. Second, we can offer compensatory strategies for children who struggle with memory tasks. Here are a few working memory boosters to use with young children:

- **Play memory games.** Games are a fun and easy way to engage children in practicing memory skills. Card games are great for improving working memory. Simple games such as Crazy Eights, Uno, and Go Fish help children practice keeping the rules of the game in their minds as they play and remembering which cards they have and which cards other people have played. Matching games support visual memory and can offer new vocabulary for young children to practice. Verbal memory games (for example, word repetition games) also support working memory and offer opportunities to practice listening and speaking skills. Using games as a means of practicing cognitive skills makes learning engaging and easily accessible for children on different academic levels. Games can also support social skills, impulse control, and language development and provide a great opportunity for skill building in a variety of domains.

- **Use clear and simple language.** Use precise and specific language when making requests or explaining next steps in a project. This will support children in being able to complete the task and feel successful while doing it.

- **Teach visualizations.** Ask children to make pictures in their heads of what they have read or heard. Have them mentally draw a picture of what they need for a specific task. This is an easy thing to incorporate into play-based classroom environments where children have a lot of time to come up with and implement their ideas. Imagine that a child comes to you saying they would like to create a circus. Rather than simply pulling down your clown costumes and finding your lion and elephant stuffed animals, ask them to draw or write out what they need for their circus—what are the elements they need to create their circus the way they hope?

- **Make it multisensory.** When children are offered several ways to process information, it can help both their working memory and the ability to transfer information into their long-term memory. Here are a few ways to use multisensory strategies to support memory:

  - Have children write down tasks.

- Toss a beanbag back and forth as new concepts are practiced (for example, math facts).

- Have children talk about their learning or repeat what is said back to you.

- Demonstrate the task before the class and use pictures to support verbal information.

For children whose working memories seem to hinder their learning, compensatory strategies can offer needed supports in the classroom so they can be successful:

- **Break down information.** Too much information all at once can overwhelm children who struggle with working memory. Offering smaller chunks of information can give children the time they need to successfully complete each task. In the classroom, there are often multistep daily tasks such as putting shoes or coats on and then lining up by the door to go outside for recess. For children with working memory challenges, breaking up these tasks can make them feel more successful. Providing visual cues for them to follow can also cut down on the adult talking time and support children in feeling independent. Not only are these strategies successful in supporting children whose working memory has been impaired by trauma, but they can also benefit children of a variety of abilities and learning styles in being successful in early childhood classrooms.

- **Build routines and reduce distractions.** Structured daily routines will help children know what to expect, minimizing the amount of new information they need to process as they move through their day. Reducing background noise and distractions can help children keep their attention on the task at hand because they are not having to process and filter out as much information.

- **Offer time for repetition.** Children with working memory issues will need more time to repeat new tasks than other children.

- **Use group work.** By working in pairs or groups, children learn from their peers, allowing them to move through tasks without needing a teacher's help.

- **Encourage children to ask for help.** Remind children that they can always ask for help or for information to be repeated.

- **Teach calming skills.** Stress and anxiety can hinder children's working memory. Chapter 7 contains multiple calming strategies that can be used to keep children calm and ready to learn.

- **Slow down.** Speak slowly and encourage children to take their time.

When working with children in play-based classrooms, it is particularly important to notice children's capacity to utilize their working memory, because sometimes children's need for support can get lost in the shuffle. If a child seems to be aimlessly walking around the classroom during open play or center time, pay attention to this behavior and find some compensatory strategies (like using visual cues or pairing the child up with a friend) so they can get the structure they need to be successful.

Attentiveness

Children who have experienced trauma may have a hard time focusing in the classroom because of their overwhelming feelings of anxiety and fear. They may be continually preoccupied with worries about their own and others' safety. If children do not feel safe, it may be impossible for them to focus on anything besides figuring out how to be safe. As children are working to keep themselves safe in the classroom, they may get lost in irrelevant details. They may have a hard time distinguishing between what is scary and what is not. Sensory integration issues may also interfere with children's capacities to focus their attention on one task.

Both hypervigilance and sensory overload can disrupt children's learning and cause their bodies to feel out of control. For example, it is circle time in a classroom, and the teacher is reading all of the children a book. The students are focused and excited to learn what will happen in the story, but as the story is read, another teacher pops her head into the classroom, sees that the class is in the middle of an activity, and leaves again. This may seem like an innocuous moment for most of the children, but for one in particular, Gem, it is overwhelming. Gem spent her first nine months living in an orphanage, where she never knew when she would be fed or changed and was often left without receiving the care and nurturance she needed to feel safe. So when new people walk into her classroom, her mind lights up with questions: *Why did the teacher enter? What did she need? Is everything okay? Am I safe?* Gem may suddenly lose interest in the story. She may have a hard time sitting still or keeping her body calm, and her world may once again feel unsafe. She may not be able to focus on the story because she is focusing intently on her teacher's mood: *Is my teacher now angry? Did something happen in the exchange between those two adults?* Gem is using the skills she learned during her earliest months living with insecurity to figure out how to keep her body and mind safe. Her inability to focus and constant hypervigilance can cause her to lose valuable academic learning time, which she needs to grow and develop at the same rate as her peers.

The Teacher's Role: Supporting Children's Capacity for Focused Attention

Children's ability to focus their attention on one task is one of the primary predictors of school success. As discussed, hypervigilance and sensory overload can undermine children's focus and learning. To support children in focusing their attention on a task, it is important to offer them opportunities to follow their own interests. Play-based and constructivist environments allow children to explore ideas, themes, and learning opportunities that matter to them, all while ensuring that the important academic concepts are being mastered. By asking questions, offering a variety of materials, and making sure that learning opportunities are relevant to their own lives, we can support children in paying attention. Children who are hypervigilant may find their attention divided as they scan the environment and other people to ensure their own safety. To reduce some of this hypervigilance, teachers can implement some of the social-emotional skills described in chapter 7 to support children in calming their bodies and minds. By allowing children to follow their own interests while simultaneously holding clear and consistent boundaries, we can give children the opportunity to safely explore and grow.

Cognitive Flexibility

In the classroom, delayed cognitive skills can present as behavioral issues as well as academic struggles. Impulsivity can be the result of impaired executive functioning, as the ability to plan, organize, delay gratification, and control behavior can be hindered by children's impulsive responses to stimuli. Deficits in children's executive functioning can lead to increased aggression and defiance.

Further, children who have a hard time expressing *cognitive flexibility*—the capacity to think about multiple concepts at once and adapt their behavior to different settings—may have a hard time regulating, which may in turn disrupt academic progress. For example, five-year-old Tomás really wants to play basketball with his friends at school. As soon as recess begins, he runs out to the basketball court to start playing, but none of his friends are there. He looks over at the grassy field and sees his friends beginning to form teams to play soccer. Tomás does not want to play and was not expecting to play soccer; he wants to play basketball. He begins pacing around the basketball court, bouncing the ball with force. He is mad now and begins to grumble about how his friends are no good anyway. Tomás is struggling with being flexible in his thinking. He had it in his mind that he would play basketball at recess, and he cannot look beyond his original plan to find a different option.

Children who lack cognitive flexibility struggle to cope with change and new information within the classroom environment as well as out in the world. Many children who live in fear-filled environments harness cognitive inflexibility as a safety mechanism; they are overly controlling and rigid in their thinking in an attempt to have some control over lives that feel out of control. Children may be misdiagnosed with mental health disorders such as oppositional defiant disorder when they are simply having trouble calming their fears.

Poor cognitive flexibility can have a negative impact not only on behavior but also on reading, writing, and math skills. Rigid thinking can make learning to read a challenge; children may struggle to understand the correct pronunciation of words and may interpret text in a literal manner. Writing can also be difficult for rigid thinkers because flexibility is required to add details, write supporting sentences, and edit for errors. These skills necessitate that children be able to shift gears as they go, something that can be challenging for children who are cognitively inflexible. Math also requires flexible thinking, as it involves adapting and looking for different strategies to answer a problem. If children get fixed on a certain formula or thought process, math can be quite challenging. Children who have experienced trauma may get stuck in rigid thinking and need support to incorporate small doses of flexibility into their thinking to learn that they can be flexible and safe at the same time.

The Teacher's Role: Supporting Cognitive Flexibility

Cognitive flexibility is a vital component in children's success in classroom environments. Children who struggle with cognitive flexibility can experience challenges in both the social-emotional and academic realms. Fortunately, there are strategies teachers can implement to support children in developing cognitive flexibility:

- **Play games.** Games offer wonderful opportunities for flexible thinking. Games that are built solely on chance, such as flipping coins, Candy Land, or Chutes and Ladders build flexibility. Of course, many children who find cognitive flexibility challenging may not initially find board games fun or interesting, so they may need teacher support and coaching as they learn how to build their capacity for flexibility.

- **Read books.** Read and discuss books that have characters with both "good" and "bad" qualities: books about robbers that steal, but only to feed their families, or books about characters that have no friends and then learn to love. This gives children opportunities to see that there is gradation in behavior and thinking.

- **Offer open-ended activities.** Create open-ended activities for children to explore that have no right or wrong answer. Painting, exploring light and shadow, and playing in the sand are all examples of activities that are flexible and open-ended. There is no correct way to engage with the materials and no set result.

- **Teach problem solving.** When conflicts arise, or a child gets stuck working through a problem, teach problem-solving skills. Asking children to think of multiple solutions to one problem teaches children how to be flexible, which in turn creates less frustration and builds capacity to manage unexpected change.

- **Allow for flexibility.** While routine and rhythm are important, it is also important to create opportunities for children to be flexible within the routine. Your daily schedule may consistently move from one set activity to the next (for example, morning meeting to centers to snack), but there can be flexibility within that rhythm.

This flexibility can be as simple as allowing the children to choose the songs they sing at morning meeting or which center they want to explore.

■ **Model flexibility.** To teach flexibility, we can model how to be flexible in the classroom. If you have a specific plan for an activity and one of the children suggests a change to the activity, be flexible and make the change if it makes sense to do so! When this happens, use language that demonstrates that you are being flexible ("I can be flexible about this") so the children are learning to match vocabulary with the action. Of course, it is important to weigh the need for a consistent routine with the need to demonstrate flexibility in your classroom, so demonstrating flexibility can start off with very small tasks, such as choosing to read two books instead of one. Teachers can demonstrate flexibility in their classrooms by proposing and utilizing different ways to do something, say something, or use something. This shows children how to be flexible as well as the value in flexibility.

■ **Acknowledge flexibility.** Notice flexibility in children's behavior and thinking. Acknowledging their flexibility will allow children to see themselves as flexible, and they will learn the language surrounding flexible thinking: "Wow, Tomás! I know you were really hoping to play basketball, but today you were flexible and decided to play soccer with the rest of your class. It looked like you had fun playing soccer!"

Conclusion

By finding tools to support young children's cognitive development, we are able to support their academic progress as well as their sense of themselves as capable and competent learners. To reach and help heal the whole child requires that we must see who they are with open hearts and minds; we need to believe in their capacity for change and their innate goodness. Jennifer is doing her very best in the classroom right now, and with the right relationship-based interventions and supportive responses to her developmental differences, she can both feel better about herself and do even better academically. We must trust that we can make the classroom a more welcoming and supportive place for all of the Jennifers of the world if we expect to change the dynamics within our own classrooms.

Expression of Trauma in the Classroom

Language Development

José Luis is three years old and until recently lived with his mom, dad, and two older brothers. José's dad was recently arrested for identity theft and will be spending the next three to five years in prison. While José's mom is sad her husband was arrested, she is also feeling relief because José's dad had recently started using drugs and was becoming increasingly erratic and violent at home. José has just started preschool, and while he seems to understand a lot of what is said to him, he still primarily grunts and points to communicate his needs. His mom has not been too worried about his slow language development, but she is hoping preschool helps him catch up.

Maltreatment in early childhood can result in comprehensive language deficits as well as more specific language difficulties that can interfere with learning, as so much of the classroom environment is centered on language acquisition and expression through oral communication, reading, and writing. These language difficulties can also lead to challenges with expressing needs and feelings effectively and understanding and conveying abstract concepts, which are critical for higher-level literacy and learning. Further, these difficulties can hinder children's behavioral and social-emotional skill development and make both reading and writing difficult (Spratt et al. 2012).

The Effect of Trauma on Language Development

Children who have experienced maltreatment can have biochemical and structural changes in their brains that lead to language delays. While of course not all children with language delays have experienced trauma, early trauma can influence language development. Learning language begins prebirth, as fetuses learn the sounds and speech patterns of their mothers in utero. Typically developing newborns come into the world prepared to process and react to sounds and, from early on, prefer the voices of their mothers. Research shows a newborn's brain responds differently to their mother's voice compared to the voice of a female stranger (Moon, Zernzach, and Kuhl 2015; Newman, Sivaratnam, and Komiti 2015). From the first days of life, children are learning language through one-on-one interactions with their primary caregivers. Through these relationships, they are learning about sounds and cadence as well as the ways in which language is used in connection with others.

Like all development, language acquisition occurs through relationships. It is through interactions that children learn how language is used on a social level. Children learn the meaning of important preverbal skills, such as gestures, facial expressions, joint attention (when people focus their attention on the same thing at the same time), and eye movements (making eye contact or not), through connection with their caregivers. These are the early skills that prepare children to communicate and talk within their first two years of life. To ensure language development, infants and young children need adults who consistently and frequently communicate with them through different modalities: talking, signing, singing, reading, listening, and playing are a few examples of ways to build comprehensive vocabularies that allow for rich understanding of language (Spratt et al. 2012).

Children who experience trauma may not have the healthy and consistent caregiving they need to learn important preverbal or verbal language skills, which can cause delays and gaps in communication. Young children who live with toxic stress may not have the capacity to attend to the speech of their primary caregiver because their bodies and minds are focused on keeping themselves safe. Similarly children who do not have an attuned and attentive caregiver may not have an opportunity to focus joint attention on specific objects or experiences, giving them fewer opportunities for learning about the environment around them. When a caregiver holds an infant close to a blooming rose and offers time to talk about the rose's color, shape, and smell, the caregiver is offering an opportunity to share an experience with the child, creating closeness between them and offering language to describe what is being seen and smelled. The infant is being exposed to and learning the words *rose, pink, sweet,* and *smell.*

Language is one of our primary modes of thinking and expressing our thinking. Research indicates that children who have experienced trauma and show symptoms of PTSD may have lower verbal scores on standardized tests than their peers (Saigh et al. 2006). Neglect is the form of trauma that is most closely connected to language delays; however, all forms of trauma can lead to underdeveloped or restricted language capacities (Spratt et al. 2012). As Cook, Blaustein, Spinazzola, and van der Kolk (2003) explain, "Children living with unpredictable violence and repeated abandonment often fail to develop appropriate language and verbal processing abilities. They then cope with threatening events and feelings of helplessness by restricting their processing of what is happening around them. Thus, these children are repeatedly unable to organize a coherent response to challenging events in their lives and instead act with disorganization" (9). Children who have experienced trauma can have delays in receptive, expressive, and general language development.

Receptive Language Development

Receptive language is the ability to understand language. It involves understanding the words, sentences, gestures, and meaning of what is said or read. Receptive language involves the actual words that are said but also the environmental cues that can help children understand what is happening. When José's teacher says, "It is almost the end of our class period together," he is expected to use his receptive language skills to understand the words said by the teacher. In the same vein, when the teacher starts to clean up the art materials and wash the tables, José's receptive language skills are expected to begin to help him understand from the visual information given that the class period is almost over. Children who have experienced trauma may find it difficult to understand nonverbal social cues and body language because understanding body language is something that occurs through practice, learned while in communication and relationship with others. For children who have not had consistent communication, this skill may be delayed or lacking (Sylvestre, Bussières, and Bouchard 2015).

Children who have experienced trauma may have delays in their processing time as they try to make meaning of the words and gestures around them.

Further, trauma can lead to children having challenges understanding abstraction, such as sarcasm and indirect commands. Indirect commands ask the listener to focus on the content of what someone is saying rather than the specific words they use. For example, a teacher may inadvertently confuse a child who has difficulty with abstraction by using an indirect command, such as, "It's time to sit down," rather than a direct command, such as "Sit down, please." Therefore, children who have experienced trauma may seem like they are not complying or having difficulty following directions when in fact they are simply having difficulty understanding what they are supposed to do (Saigh et al. 2006).

The Teacher's Role: Supporting Receptive Language Development

Teachers can have a significant impact on young children's language development. Attending high-quality early education programs can enhance children's vocabulary, language comprehension, and communication skills. Educators can support young children's delayed language skills by using relational and intentional techniques. First and foremost, children who have survived trauma need to feel that the classroom is safe and predictable before they can be calm enough to complete higher-level thinking skills (see chapter 7 for whole-classroom strategies that create the predictability and safety children need to feel calm). The following strategies can be used to engage children in enhancing their receptive language skills—and, importantly, many will also enhance children's expressive language skills as well (see pages 78–83).

- **Practice continuity of care.** Babies need a lot of time to watch and listen to their caregivers talk. For babies who have experienced neglect or relational trauma, looking too long at someone's face may cause fear and uncertainty. These babies may look away and try to avoid engaging in close communication. Practicing continuity of care, where the same caregivers consistently care for the same children, develops deep relationships between babies and caregivers. This allows teachers to build consistent, predictable, and nurturing relationships with children who have experienced trauma, supporting them in feeling safe in their relationship and being open to looking at and listening to their caregivers.

- **Engage in joint attention with children.** Children who experience relational trauma may not get many experiences engaging in joint attention with a supportive adult. As discussed earlier in this chapter, joint attention is the capacity to follow another person's focus of attention and direct someone else's attention to where you are interested. This early communication encourages caregivers to engage with children and name objects and events for them. For children who have experienced trauma, not engaging in joint attention means they are getting fewer opportunities to share their wants, needs, and interests through pointing, gestures, and words. Trauma-responsive educators need to be responsive to children's interests and questions. When a child is pointing and grunting, simply instructing, "Use your words," may not work if they do not have the words. By engaging in joint attention and saying something like, "I see you looking at the big red fire truck parked across the street—it's taller than both of us!" the child is learning new vocabulary and building a connection with a safe caregiver.

- **Get on their level.** Being face-to-face with young children when you talk to them allows them to watch how our mouths form words and learn from our facial expressions.

- **Talk with children more.** For children like José who live with a lot of chaos, their families may not have the energy or time to spend a lot of time communicating with them at home. The more we intentionally offer them opportunities to engage with us as teachers, the more direct time they will have to practice appropriate social communication skills.

- **Offer children more information about objects, emotions, and events.** Many children come into the classroom with limited understanding about the world outside of their own experiences. Offer more information about objects, emotions, and events as a way to scaffold their learning and offer them new understandings.

- **Check in often to make sure they understand you.** Just as it is important to offer children more information, it is important to recognize that many children may not know all the vocabulary words you expect from a child their age, and that they need you to check in to make sure they know and understand the words you are using. For example, Teacher Tanh is teaching second graders about money. They have reviewed the names and worth of each coin and bill, and now they are working on adding and subtracting different amounts of money. To support them in their learning, Teacher Tanh has set up a market, complete with vegetables and fruits to buy. However, for Kay and Lee, twins in the classroom who have experienced severe neglect, these fruits and vegetables are blobs they have seen in the grocery store or at friends' houses; they do not have any vocabulary to describe what they are. Ensuring that all the children know the basic vocabulary you plan to use in your lessons will help everyone be on equal footing as they engage in their learning.

■ **Choose diverse materials.** Ensure that the materials, furnishings, toys, and foods in your classroom reflect the children's cultures and home languages so they can identify with the images, words, and music they hear as well as see themselves within the classroom community. This will make it easier to pick up on the context and nonverbal clues that help them understand what is being communicated.

■ **Play games.** Find games that involve listening and speaking where children can practice their skills in a nonjudgmental and fun environment. There is an endless number of fun listening games out there. Here are a few popular games that can be used with preschoolers and elementary-age children:

- *Telephone:* Sit in a circle and whisper a message to the first child, who passes the message to the next, and so on. The last person states the message out loud to the group. Typically the message has changed dramatically from its original form and hilarity ensues.

- *Freeze Dance:* Have children dance along to the music and freeze their bodies when the music stops. This is a great game for controlling impulses as well.

- *The People Say:* This game requires listening for a certain phrase, "The people say," and moving only when the leader includes this phrase. For example, the leader says, "The people say . . . touch your nose," and the group members touch their noses. Every once in a while, the group leader gives a command without first saying, "The people say," which the group is supposed to ignore. This game can be played in a noncompetitive way in which participants are not "out" for making mistakes but instead just try again the next round. This is another game that supports impulse control.

- *Red Light, Green Light:* In this game a leader calls out "red light" or "green light." When the leader calls "green light," it means it's time to run; when they call "red light," it is time to stop. The goal is to reach the leader while listening. There are several variations to the game to add different body movements (see chapter 6 for the importance of physical and sensory development): add colors to mean different movements (yellow light can mean skip, blue light can mean hop), or add colors to mean different animal walks (yellow light can mean crab walk, blue light can mean bear crawl).

■ **Listen for sounds.** Listen to different sounds and talk about what you hear together.

■ **Use visual cues.** For children who are delayed in their language development, visual cues can support their understanding of what is happening in the classroom. Visual cues can reduce the auditory language needed to understand what is happening in the classroom as well as offer another sensory avenue for communication and connection. These can be simple drawings you create, pictures found online, or photographs of the children themselves participating in activities. You can place them around the classroom as visual reminders of the daily rhythm and transition markers or loop them together and give them to children to hold in their pockets or attach to their belts. These visual cues can be brought out and used during transitions, during conflict and problem solving, or at any other moment when children are struggling.

■ **Read.** Read, and then read some more. For children like José who are behind in their language skills, books can be magical ways to explore and expand language skills. Books offer new and engaging language to support children's vocabulary and imaginations. Ensure that the books in your classroom represent culturally diverse families and life experiences. When reading books, make sure to identify the different parts of the book: the front and back cover, title, author and illustrator, and so forth. This will allow children to familiarize themselves with the practical use of books.

- **Tell stories, sing songs, and do lots of fingerplays and puppet shows.** Finding different ways to engage in language throughout the day will offer children many opportunities to learn. Some children may not have the attention span necessary to sit through a whole book but love the rhythm and movement that goes along with songs or fingerplays. Other children may have a hard time simply listening to oral stories but love to watch as characters come alive through puppet shows. Children learn in different ways, and by engaging in multiple avenues to increase language development, we are offering all children, but especially children who have experienced trauma, more ways to learn.

- **Anticipate triggers.** By three months, a baby can recognize sounds associated with different situations—running water means it's bath time, and barking means their dog is close. For infants who have experienced trauma, this also means that by three months sounds and experiences in the classroom can trigger their stress response. Teachers must be aware of the ways infants and babies react to different sounds and situations in the classroom and respond appropriately. Continuing activities when children are clearly overwhelmed, either shut down or screaming, and hoping they learn to handle the activities will not work for young children who have experienced trauma. Children need to experience being calm as much as possible.

Expressive Language Development

Expressive language is the ability to communicate with others through words, sentences, body movements, and writing. Expressive language is vitally important for young children because it allows for healthy development and communication of social-emotional needs. Expressive language allows children to share their thoughts and feelings, wants and needs, and ideas. Expressive language is needed for all higher-level academic work in which speaking and writing are used to communicate learned topics.

Children who have experienced trauma may not have the expressive language skills necessary to negotiate, problem solve, and maintain intelligible narrative dialogue, which makes communication with others challenging and can inhibit relationship building and connection with friends and teachers. Trauma can cause children to have difficulty conveying abstract thoughts, which is important for higher-level literacy skills. Many children who have experienced neglect or physical abuse may not have the language necessary to express their feelings and understand what is happening in their bodies when they have big feelings. This can cause confusion, sadness, and anger in young children (Spratt et al. 2012; Sylvestre, Bussières, and Bouchard 2015).

Many children who have experienced trauma have delays in both their receptive and expressive language processing, and it can take them more time to understand and respond to verbal questions. Slow receptive and expressive language development can lead to behavioral challenges within an educational environment and across the life-span (Cook et al. 2003; Spratt et al. 2012). A two-thousand-participant study from Northwestern University found that children between twelve and thirty-eight months with expressive language delays were twice as likely to have frequent and long-lasting temper tantrums compared to their peers with typical language development (Manning et al. 2019). Behavioral challenges connected to language development can arise because children are not able to understand or communicate their thoughts and feelings, and because they feel badly about themselves when they do not understand the concepts that are being communicated in school.

Language delays can cause embarrassment and anxiety in young children who realize that what they are trying to say does not always get communicated in an effective way. For example, let's take Jennifer, who we learned about in chapter 4. Jennifer has found it difficult to make friends other than her one good friend, Susan, whom she has known for most of her life. One thing she has noticed is that peers sometimes seem to have a hard time understanding her, and she has been told she's "weird" by more than one child in her class. Jennifer does not think she's weird, and she doesn't understand why Susan seems to be able to decipher what she is saying but other children cannot. Often Jennifer has a hard time expressing herself, and when she gets excited, it becomes even harder, which is frustrating for her. For example, during recess one day, a bunch of her peers were comparing the sizes of their feet and trading shoes; Jennifer put her foot next to Susan's and said, "Susan's foot is way too shorter." One of her peers looked at her and laughed while saying, "That doesn't even make sense!" which embarrassed Jennifer immensely. Luckily for Jennifer, Susan jumped in and said, "Oh, you know what she means—my foot is smaller. We can never share shoes." Jennifer was embarrassed and also did not truly understand what she had said wrong; she did not have the expressive language skills to understand her grammatical errors. Still flustered by the interaction, Jennifer went inside after recess for her favorite class, art. During class her art teacher, Ms. Sanchez, asked Jennifer to fill the sink basin with water to soak their used paintbrushes. Jennifer happily went over to fill the sink basin but realized the stopper was broken, so the water was draining rather than pooling up the way she wanted. She turned to her art teacher for help and said, "Ms. Sanchez, the sink keeps on drowning each of the ones." This caused the other children to burst into laughter. Again Jennifer was embarrassed and confused; she did not know what she had said wrong and did not know how to fix it. However, Susan knew exactly what Jennifer meant and hopped up, saying, "I know what she means—I can help her fix it!" and ran over to help her stop the sink. These types of situations can make children like Jennifer feel less confident in connecting with peers or speaking up in class. It lowers their self-esteem and makes them hesitant to try new activities or reach out to others in more meaningful ways.

Language development is connected to many academic areas. Of these, the most important may be reading and writing. Research demonstrates that receptive and expressive vocabulary skills affect the development of both phonological and word-identification skills (Duplechain, Reigner, and Packard 2008).

Children who have experienced abuse and neglect are at risk for continued impaired language development. The good news is that access to the relationship-based interactions and linguistic opportunities necessary for optimal language skills can help offset these delays. Repeated language exposure is necessary to learn new words and appropriate contexts for word placement. Teachers must understand the importance of connection and relationships in building children's language capacities and their ability to understand and express complex linguistic concepts.

The Teacher's Role: Supporting Expressive Language Development

Infants, toddlers, and some preschoolers who have experienced trauma may not have the relationship-based prelanguage experiences they need to be primed for talking. As early childhood educators, we have the extraordinary opportunity to shape their language development by being an attuned, calm, and safe adult to communicate with and learn from. Here are some strategies for supporting children in learning these foundational skills:

- **Communicate through turn-taking.** Turn-taking in communication typically develops within the first few weeks of life. As babies make noises and movements, their trusted adults interpret the baby's noises and respond with sounds, words, or actions. Children who have experienced trauma may not have experience with the expected call and response babies need for healthy communication, and they may come into the classroom without typical communication patterns. To help babies learn the back-and-forth that typically occurs in conversations, teachers can leave gaps in their talking for babies to respond. Eventually this will lead to babies and their teachers taking turns with sounds, actions, and eventually words.

- **Respond to children's vocalizations and speech.** Connected to the idea of turn-taking, we must respond to children's vocalizations and speech as they occur. This teaches children that we care about who they are and what they have to say. For children who have experienced early trauma or neonatal drug exposure, much of their vocalizations and speech may involve screaming or expressing distress. In this context, responding calmly and with attuned attention may feel overwhelming for some caregivers. Communicating within the teaching team and practicing good self-care (see chapter 8) can support everyone in remaining calm, and appropriately and effectively responding to children.

- **Use soft eyes and smiles.** Because babies from an early age begin to search faces looking for clues about how people feel and how those feelings translate into specific behaviors, we must be very aware of the ways we look at young children, especially when we are feeling frustrated. We must always work to look at babies and older children with *soft eyes*, eyes that communicate love and respect. Babies typically begin to smile around six weeks, and this initiation of warm interaction from babies fosters social communication. Research demonstrates that adults tend to initiate more communication with responsive babies. However, young children who have experienced trauma may be delayed in smiling and early babbles, so as trauma-responsive educators, it is important to be aware of these possible delays and continue to foster social interactions with babies even if big smiles and engaged responses are not happening, while being mindful of not overwhelming them.

As children grow and develop, many of the strategies mentioned earlier continue to support healthy expressive language development. Here are some strategies for supporting preschoolers and elementary-age children's communication skills once some speaking skills have developed:

- **Elicit conversations with children.** By asking children questions and initiating conversations with them, we are demonstrating care about who they are and what they have to say. This can be a powerful way for children to feel seen and heard.

- **Extend children's language.** Take the language children are using and extend it as a way of modeling language use. For example, if a child yells, "Kitty!" the teacher can say, "Yes, there is an orange kitty sitting on top of a car outside." Teachers can also add new words and expand young children's grammar. For example, if a child says, "Big truck!" the adult can respond with, "Yes, look at that big blue truck coming down the road."

- **Create a culturally diverse environment.** Use books, music, and other materials that reflect the diversity of the children and families in the classroom. This offers a rich source of vocabulary and can support all children in feeling like a part of the classroom community.

- **Encourage family involvement.** Encourage families to share music, songs, and stories that they love to sing or hear in their homes.

- **Engage in conversations about things that matter to children.** One of the best ways to connect with children is by engaging in conversations about things that matter to them. Strengthening these relationships supports children in feeling calm and remaining in the learning zone. By following their lead and interests, we can ask questions and wonder with them as they expand their knowledge and understanding.

- **Engage children in new experiences.** For children who have limited experiences, bringing in objects they may not have seen before or taking field trips to new places can expand their understanding about the world and offer them new vocabulary.

- **Talk about feelings.** Children with language delays are more likely to have behavioral concerns in the classroom, so offering language to communicate feelings will help them express big emotions in a different way. See chapter 7 for strategies on teaching feelings.

Supporting Children in Hearing You

As discussed previously, children with trauma histories may have auditory processing issues. They may not remember accurately what is said to them, and they may not be able to place it in context and remember it for a typical length of time (which for young children is often a short amount of time). For many children, picking out and understanding the important words in a conversation may be difficult, but this can be especially challenging for children who have experienced trauma. Their brains may take longer to process words, and they may get overwhelmed easily. They need deliberate communication and consistent repetition of words and experiences to begin to form connections about how the world works. To support young children who have experienced trauma, we must be precise with our words and our intentions. Here are a few tips for speaking to children who may have auditory processing issues:

- Speak slowly.

- Choose your words wisely and sparingly.

- Say the most important part right away—they may only hear the beginning.

- Connect the most important point to the big picture: "Stop. I will not let you hit." "Ouch! That hurt, Sammy. I need your friends to feel safe in the classroom."

- Use five words or less when a child is escalated—children cannot process more than five words at a time when their brains are overwhelmed.

Supporting Children in Learning the Language of Hope

Many of the children we work with who have experienced trauma live in environments where they see little hope for their futures. We can offer them the language of hope as a means of expanding their vocabulary around what they expect of the world and of themselves, and also as a means of supporting their sense of self as a person who is worthy of good things. Here are some helpful phrases adapted from a list written by Deborah Gray (2012) that can be used to support young children's sense of hope:

- *"That was a thoughtful thing to say."* This offers an opportunity to compliment their words and thinking.

- *"You have a strong sense of fairness."* This phrase can work very well for children who struggle with feeling like things are constantly unfair, or if they try to control the behavior of other children.

- *"You really care about your friends."* For children who have a hard time staying safe with their words or bodies, pointing out moments when you feel like they really show they care can be helpful.

- *"I believe in you."* This phrase demonstrates that a child's momentary behavior does not detract from your love and positive regard.

- *"I liked how you did that. Wow!"* Small acts of showing wonder and amazement at a child's abilities can fill them up with good feelings about themselves that they may not be getting other places. For children who do not learn as babies and young children that they are seen and heard and that other people delight in them, our language as educators can go a long way to offering them that feeling of being fully seen. Showing your joy for what they do is different than simply saying, "Good job" or "Way to go," which ends up being unnecessary and lacking substance.

- *"Wow, look what you made!"* This allows children to reflect on their own abilities and to feel proud of what they are capable of accomplishing.

- *"You were being so careful with that tool! That will keep your friends so safe."* This offers children an opportunity both to see their own skills and to notice how their behavior can positively influence others.

- *"I can't help but find you lovable."* This phrase shows the child that they have intrinsic worth.

Conclusion

Language delays can frustrate young children and hinder both the social and academic aspects of school. Children who have experienced trauma need support in learning and using language so they can feel confident and a sense of belonging in the classroom. Trauma-responsive educators can use the techniques listed in this chapter to build confidence in children who have experienced trauma. Of course, some language challenges extend beyond what educators can do on their own in the classroom, and when outside support is needed, it is important to consult with speech pathologists (see chapter 8) and other specialists who specifically work on enhancing language development. Because developmental domains do not exist in a vacuum, there are many strategies listed in other chapters of this book that also support language development. By offering children comprehensive trauma-responsive environments, we can support their whole beings.

Expression of Trauma in the Classroom

Physical Development

————————————

Marie is six months old and living in her third foster home. She was removed from her parents' care at birth and spent two weeks in an emergency foster home before moving to her cousin's home. However, just one month later, her cousin called Marie's caseworker and told her she was not able to continue fostering. Her cousin already had four children and just did not have the capacity or support to take on one more child. Marie moved again to a nonrelative foster care placement, where she has been for the past four months. Her current foster parents work full-time, so Marie is in child care full-time. Although every day she seems more and more relaxed, both at home and at school, she is still fairly shut down. She is just now starting to bat at toys and trying to grip them in her hands. She is not yet rolling and seems perfectly content lying on her back. Marie's teachers are beginning to worry that she is developing a flat spot on the back of her head, so they are both holding her and putting her on her tummy more to help her experience the world from different positions.

Young children like Marie who have experienced trauma may experience biological changes and delays in their physical development, including their fine-motor, gross-motor, and sensory skills. They may have trouble with coordination, balance, body tone, movement, and understanding their own strength (Stephens 2018). When children experience early neglectful or scary environments, their bodies, brains, and immune systems may not develop as expected. Children need engaging social environments to support them in learning to roll, crawl, walk, run, write, and speak. The following sections will discuss some ways in which children's bodies can be affected by early trauma.

Physical Development

Early trauma can change children's physical developmental trajectories. We have eight senses that influence how we respond to and perceive the world: visual (what we see), auditory (what we hear), tactile (what we touch), olfactory (what we smell), gustatory (what we taste), vestibular (how we sense our body's movements, position, and balance), proprioceptive (how we perceive our bodies in space), and interoceptive (how we feel our bodies' sensations). Each of these senses helps us feel aware of our surroundings and our internal states (Stephens 2018; Stock Kranowitz 2006).

Starting in utero, children's sensory systems may change due to trauma and other early experiences. The brain stem plays a significant role in the body's ability to process stimuli. Because the brain stem is primarily developed in utero, prenatal alcohol or drug use and traumatic experiences can affect children's sensory systems, resulting in children being oversensitive or undersensitive to incoming stimuli. Once a child is born, early deprivation and neglect can also negatively impact sensory processing, which causes trouble analyzing, organizing, and responding to sensations. Children who have a hard time recognizing and integrating stimuli can end up having trouble regulating their feelings and behaviors because the stimuli can cause them to over- or underreact to everyday experiences (Purvis et al. 2013; Stephens 2018).

Children who experience maltreatment prenatally, as newborns, or shortly thereafter have a high likelihood of being overwhelmed by the traumas they experience. Living in a chaotic environment full of *sounds* such as screaming, fighting, or the silence of being alone; *smells* of drug use, urine, or feces; the *sensations* of being left wet or cold; or *movements* of people fighting or the cessation of movement as adults black out from alcohol or drug use can cause young children's senses to be easily overwhelmed. When infants and young children are left to process these sensations on their own, they can be overwhelmed by the daunting task. Young children need adults to support them in processing and understanding big sensations, and without that support, young children can end up with disorganized and excessively sensitive sensory systems.

Sensory-Seeking and Sensory-Avoidant Behaviors

Children who survive maltreatment can be sensory seeking, sensory avoidant, or both, depending on the environment. Children who are *sensory seeking* will crave certain stimuli; they may be extremely interested in movement, lights, colors, sounds, smells, and tastes (Purvis et al. 2013; Stephens 2018; Stock Kranowitz 2006). Imagine four-year-old Fynn, who comes running into the classroom pushing past his peers to give his teacher a hug. He hardly seems to notice that she is in the middle of a conversation with a parent as he barrels into her, and she falls backward as the strength of his body pushes into her. Fynn does not seem to notice the force of his body or what happened to his teacher, so as they land on the ground, he looks up at her with a huge smile on his face and sweetly says, "I'm here!" Children like Fynn who are sensory seeking may try to find calm within themselves by displaying these behaviors:

- rubbing or bumping against walls or furniture
- rubbing or bumping against peers or adults
- craving touch
- chewing on their clothes, grinding their teeth
- frequently engaging in roughhouse play
- pushing, slapping, or hugging too hard
- enjoying very muddy or messy play
- enjoying being wrapped up in blankets and burrowing under weighted blankets
- dumping toys and rummaging through them without clear intent
- licking or tasting inedible objects long past the developmentally typical window
- constantly moving, fidgeting, jumping, and having a hard time staying still
- underresponding to pain
- biting or hitting themselves, banging their heads
- overstuffing their mouths when eating

- craving spicy, salty, or sour foods

- pushing too hard with their pencil so they are constantly breaking the tip, or not pushing hard enough and having a difficult time making marks

Children who are *sensory avoidant*, on the other hand, will want to avoid or get away from certain stimuli, even stimuli that are necessary for basic everyday functioning (Purvis et al. 2013; Stephens 2018). Take, for example, two-year-old Silvia, who hates to wash her hands. Before every meal and after every diaper change, each child is required to wash their hands, but Silvia tries to refuse every time. As the water hits her hands, she screams and cries, and when she is done washing, she takes a towel and wipes every last drop off her hands before returning to play. This process can take her ten to fifteen minutes to complete, but she refuses to move on until her hands are dry. Children like Silvia who are sensory avoidant may try to find calm within themselves by doing the following:

- avoiding touch, not wanting cuddles or hugs

- only wearing specific clothes (often without tags or seams)

- complaining about typical smells, sounds, and lights

- avoiding dirt, water, or any sort of mess

- avoiding grass or specific ground coverings

- avoiding playground equipment or having their feet leave the ground

- losing their balance easily, falling over, or trying to sit on a chair but missing the chair completely

- expressing fear around things that to them feel dangerous (stepping off a curb, walking on uneven ground, going down a slide)

- overresponding to pain, becoming aggressive or upset about small bumps from other children

- avoiding games and activities that necessitate touch

- complaining about wind on their faces or a small sprinkling of rain

- only eating specific foods

Children who have experienced developmental trauma may express chronic or significant physical ailments, which are somatic expressions of their trauma. Children in the classroom may complain of recurrent pains, such as headaches, stomachaches, or backaches, without a known cause. Or the opposite can be true, and they can be physically sick with a sore throat, runny nose, or fever but may not express or notice that they are feeling sick. Further, adverse childhood experiences can increase the likelihood of medical issues in children, such as asthma, skin problems, and autoimmune disorders. Chronic stress in childhood can weaken the immune system and make children susceptible to health issues throughout their lives (Burke Harris 2018). These health issues can cause children to miss valuable school time, which can have a negative impact on their academic success.

Children who have experienced trauma are too often seen as exaggerators; they are perceived as constantly making up hurt knees or itchy tags to receive attention. If their complaints are exaggerations, they deserve support in their own right, because if children are expressing a need for attention, it is our job to figure out how to offer them that attention. However, it is also likely that these children are feeling that level of physical discomfort. Children with interoceptive-system differences may have a hard time recognizing their physical bodies. This can lead to trouble recognizing when they need to use the restroom, causing them to soil themselves. They may also be chronically constipated, which can lead to enuresis. They may not be able to tell when their bodies are hungry or full, leading to not eating enough or gorging on food. And they may not recognize when their bodies are ill or hurt.

Children who experience chronic stress can be sensory seeking and sensory avoidant in different situations, and they may be hyper- or hyposensitive to touch, sounds, smells, and light (Stephens 2018). For some children, a small accidental tap from a friend while putting on coats may feel like a hard push. Their bodies are dysregulated, so they are overresponding to the sensory stimuli. The opposite may be true as well; children who experience trauma may be underresponsive to touch, pain, or their internal physical states. Without this body awareness, children who have experienced trauma may injure themselves without realizing it, which can be alarming. When a child comes to school with an extremely large bruise and no explanation of how it occurred, they may not actually remember getting hurt (Zero to Six Collaborative Group, NCTSN 2010).

Being able to understand sensory-processing challenges can allow teachers a different lens with which to see children's behaviors (Stock Kranowitz 2006). Rather than seeing a child who is constantly bumping into other children or giving hard hugs as intentionally raucous, we can see them as having a sensory need that needs to be met (Zero to Six Collaborative Group, NCTSN 2010). In chapter 8, I introduce other professionals that may be called upon to support our students who have experienced trauma, including occupational therapists who can provide sensory diets—activities specifically chosen and scheduled to support individual sensory needs (Stephens 2018).

The Teacher's Role: Supporting Sensory Development

Children need sensory-rich environments for optimal holistic development. Children should be allowed and encouraged to have varied sensory experiences, such as regular experiences with art, messy play, water play, fine-motor play, and gross-motor play (Stock Kranowitz 2006). When supporting young children who may have varying physical development needs, it is imperative that we reach out to experts such as occupational and physical therapists. They will be able to guide our process and see clearly individual students' needs as well as suggest strategies to support the whole class.

Sensory-Related Calming Techniques

Sensory-related calming techniques can be helpful in bringing awareness to young children about their bodies' responses to stress and trauma. Brain research shows us that sensory-related activities can help children shift from their stress response of fight, flight, or freeze into feeling calmer. To support young children who may be hypervigilant or hypovigilant, we can work to calm all their senses. Here are some techniques that are particularly helpful with young children, focusing on different senses.

Visual ways to create calm bodies and minds include the following:

- **Use visual cues.** Visual cues can be helpful for children who may not be able to quickly process what is said to them. Show them a picture of a mouse when they are supposed to be as quiet as a mouse, or show them a picture of a lion when they are supposed to make lots of noise.

- **Play visual games.** For children who are hypervigilant, games like I Spy can help them focus their attention and calm their bodies. Ask a child to name every red item they see in the room or to name items they see that are made out of wood. Another fun game, I Am Thinking of a Person, can support slow and purposeful transitions. After a group activity, say, "I am thinking of a person who is wearing blue," and have the other children guess who you are thinking of. Once the correct child is named, they get up to transition to the next activity. This allows children to focus their visual energy while also stopping a rush of children from transitioning all at once.

- **Use partitions.** Naptime is often a challenging time for young children who have experienced trauma. One way of supporting children in calming their bodies when they are escalated is to block out some of the visual stimulation around them. This does not mean they should be in a space where they cannot see their trusted adult—we do not want to scare them or make them feel isolated—but placing children strategically in the room where much of the visual clutter is blocked out can support them in calming their bodies and minds and falling asleep.

- **Use low or nonfluorescent lighting.** For babies who are crying, young children who are escalated, or children who had neonatal substance exposure, lighting can make all the difference. Dimming the lights or using nonfluorescent lights can create a calm environment for children.

- **Be purposeful with wall space.** Walls full of clutter can be overstimulating for children of all ages. Colorful borders and vibrant posters may be fun for some of the children, but for children who have experienced trauma, all of the clutter may be overstimulating.

- **Pick neutral colors.** Paint walls calming neutral colors. Make sure the colors are light and can brighten up the space.

Noise-related ways to create calm bodies and minds include the following:

- **Use a calm voice.** Young children who have experienced trauma may be overwhelmed by loud or gruff voices. Use a calm, consistent cadence and tone to support them in learning that you are a consistent and safe person in their lives.

- **Sing.** Singing songs can be relaxing for young children who have experienced trauma. Using songs at transitional moments throughout the day can support children in learning the daily rhythm and can stop some of the fear that comes from not knowing what is next.

- **Use music and noise.** Using instrumental music, white noise, or nature sounds during resting times and calming moments throughout the day can soothe young children's escalated bodies. Create a "listening station" in your classroom to allow children to calm themselves on their own using music.

- **Use rhythm and beat.** Use rhythm and beat to calm children's bodies and get them into the learning zone. Clap, stomp, and chant to focus children's attention and attune their bodies to what is happening in the moment.

- **Allow for children's sounds.** Some children need to make sounds to feel calm. They may sigh loudly or clear their throat or just seem to always have a noise coming out of them. Remember that this may be a way they stabilize themselves and keep calm, reminding themselves and others that they exist and they matter. Allow sounds as much as you can, and eventually, with support, they will realize they do not need to constantly create noise to validate their existence.

- **Place items strategically to lessen noise in the classroom.** Many classrooms have hardwood or tile floors, which can be loud when children are building block towers, scraping chairs across the surface, and running. Bring the overall noise level in the classroom down by strategically placing rugs and soft furnishings—cushions, beanbags, and wall hangings—around the classroom.

- **Use noise-canceling headphones.** Some children who are sensitive to noise may benefit from wearing noise-canceling headphones in the classroom. This can block out or muffle some of the classroom sounds, allowing children to focus on the desired classroom activities.

Tactile ways to create calm bodies and minds include the following:

- **Use touch.** Pat or rub young children's backs or arms as a way of creating connection and comfort. When using touch-related soothing techniques, it is always important to remember young children's individual stories; for some children who have experienced sexual abuse or physical abuse, touch can be overwhelming and upsetting. We must be tuned in to the needs of the children we work with to know which strategies will work for which children. For children who respond well to touch, it can be an effective and powerful way to calm them.

- **Create specific touch.** Some children who have experienced physical abuse or neglect equate touch with trauma. As I discussed earlier, they may arch away or try to avoid your touch. Creating a specific touch by touching a baby or young child in the same place in the same way every time you initiate touch can allow them to begin to associate your touch with a calming, positive experience distinct from their previous experiences.

- **Tell babies and children before you pick them up.** Magda Gerber, the founder of the Resources for Infant Educators (RIE) philosophy, believed that all babies deserve the respect of being told what is going to happen to their bodies. By simply stating, "I am going to pick you up now," before picking up a child, we can communicate respect for their bodies and their needs (Gerber and Johnson 1998).

- **Use infant massage.** With training, infant massage can reduce crying and fussiness, help sleep, and alleviate constipation. Direct touch is a very powerful way to connect with infants.

- **Set up sensory activities or stations.** Sensory activities can calm young children. Demonstrate how to run your hands through a water tray or sensory table. Offer playdough, sand trays, squeeze balls, and Silly Putty to squish, push, and roll. Offer quiet spaces for these activities where children can calm themselves and get away from some of the more vigorous play occurring in the classroom.

- **Play tactile games.** Touch-related games can be a great way to integrate a small amount of touch into the day for children who may find touch overwhelming: Patty Cake or Runny Mousey are good games for this. Runny Mousey involves starting by a child's toes and slowly crawling your fingers up their leg while saying, "Walking mousey, walking mousey," and then switching to quickly moving your fingers up their stomachs and onto their heads, saying, "Running mousey, running mousey." This is often a favorite in toddler classrooms. It is important to use good firm touch while playing the game so as not to tickle. It can bring great joy and big belly laughs. This game presents an excellent opportunity to practice consent, because before touching the child's body, you can ask, "Would you like to play Walking Mousey?" and they can say yes or no. And once you start, they can say stop at any time, and you can demonstrate how you move your hands off their body when they tell you to stop. Children can also choose where they play: a child may say, "I want to play Walking Mousey, but I do not want the mousey to go on my head." This allows children to play in a way that feels comfortable to them, without pushing them too far.

- **Offer fine-motor activities.** Lacing cards, beading, and sorting games can support children in calming their bodies as they work to sequence or create order. This can move them from the stress response into the higher-level thinking areas of their brain.

- **Provide fidgets.** Have a basket (or two!) of fidgets for the children to grab if they need something to hold during circle time or other focused periods throughout the day. Teachers often worry that if they introduce fidgets into their classrooms, all of the children will want them, and it will end up being another distraction rather than something helpful. When you first introduce fidgets into the classroom, this may in fact happen, but after a couple of weeks, the children who do not need fidgets tend to get bored of the activity, while the children who benefit from the tactile activity stick with their favorite fidgets.

- **Introduce weighted blankets, vests, or lap pillows; brushing; and deep muscle compressions.** Under the guidance of a trained occupational therapist, all of these techniques can support young children's arousal and regulation needs.

Smell-related ways to create calm bodies and minds include the following:

- **Offer calming lotions.** Lotions can be both a touch- and smell-related calming practice. Choose a few common feelings or needs that can become the names of the lotion bottles, such as "proud lotion," "sad lotion," "hurt lotion," or "love lotion." Give each lotion bottle its own smell. When children are needing extra support or are having big feelings, offer them some of the lotion. At first they may need help, so this can be an activity done together— especially when done with younger children—and as the children get older, they will be able to choose and apply the lotions on their own. Choose soothing scents to support them in feeling calm, such as lavender, geranium, or rose.

- **Have a fresh-smelling classroom.** Smells can remind children of their past experiences and can be triggering for young children who have experienced trauma. Ensure that the classroom smells fresh and clean so children know what smell to expect when they walk in.

- **Allow special lovies and blankies.** Because smells can comfort young children, allow children to keep their special items with them. These personal items can provide them with familiar smells that remind them they are safe.

- **Avoid harsh smells.** Avoid wearing perfume or cologne or smelling like smoke. Many children are sensitive to strong smells. Smells can cause headaches and nausea, which can affect young children's moods.

- **Bring in smells.** Create smelling trays of different scents (these can be made using old spice jars). These can be used as a matching game based on smell or simply as a way to allow children to use smell to calm themselves down.

Taste-related ways to create calm bodies and minds include the following:

- **Have a drink or eat a snack.** Thirst and hunger can cause huge upsets in some children. For children who have experienced food insecurity, the feeling of hunger can be very triggering. Having healthy, readily available snacks can support children in learning that they will always be fed in the classroom.

- **Use oral stimulation.** Children who have experienced trauma may want to suck on bottles, pacifiers, or their thumbs long after other children have stopped. Because trauma-informed practices are focused on connection, we never want to shame a child for these activities. In the classroom, we can offer children chew toys, chewelry, or gum, if it is developmentally appropriate, to satiate the need to suck or chew (Marchetti 2015).

- **Use taste.** Taste items that are similar and different to help children learn what they like and do not like and how to notice subtle differences; ask them to taste varieties of food to notice the similarities and dissimilarities. For example, cut up several varieties of apples or oranges and ask them to taste each one to notice the differences. Ask them to choose which ones they like. Another activity involves asking the children to try different vegetables raw and cooked. Ask questions such as "What do raw carrots taste like compared to cooked carrots?" "Which do you like more?" "What about broccoli?" These activities allow children the opportunity to understand differences, state their preferences, and make comparisons. This simple exercise can be a powerful opportunity for children who have experienced trauma to choose their own interests, likes, or desires and learn more about who they are.

Movement- and *balance-*related ways to create calm bodies and minds include the following:

- **Use co-movement.** For infants, toddlers, and young preschoolers, rocking, bouncing, swinging, and swaying can calm their bodies and help them move through big feelings.

- **Swing.** Young children from infants all the way up to eight-year-olds can experience calming by swinging. Fifteen minutes of swinging can have a six- to eight-hour effect on the brain.

- **Carry children.** Holding infants and young children or having them ride in a stroller can calm them through the slow rhythmical movement.

- **Walk.** Taking a walk with a trusted adult can be used as a calming technique for many children. For an older child who needs regular movement and walking, try assigning them a special job that involves walking from the classroom to another part of the school every day so they can get that good movement in on a regular basis.

- **Practice yoga.** The act of doing yoga as a community can allow children the physical movement they need as well as the intimacy of doing an activity as a community without the vulnerability of verbal communication.

- **Push.** Using a wall or large beanbag to push can provide the input some children need to become calm. Have children put both hands flat against the wall, shoulder-width apart (to support children who need visual cues, cut out and tape hands onto the wall where their hands should be placed). Have them extend their arms and push as hard as they can against the wall. They can also complete push-ups against the wall for a challenge.

- **Vary play equipment.** Ensure there is play equipment on the playground that allows for sensory input and integration: swings, teeter-totters, hopper balls, balancing beams, bikes, trikes, balls, and climbing structures.

- **Provide proper furniture.** Allow children to use a standing desk, exercise ball, rocking chair, or wiggle seat. This small amount of movement can center and calm children's internal systems.

- **Play movement games.** Many games integrate the body and mind, including Freeze Tag; Duck, Duck, Goose; Ring around-the-Rosie; Red Light, Green Light; and Jump and Freeze, as well as moving to music with different rhythms and tempos.

- **Play games to promote cross-lateral movement.** Games that support cross-lateral movement can calm young children's bodies. Here are a few ways to enhance cross-lateral movement and integrate bodies and minds: bear or crab crawl; move through an obstacle course; march or tiptoe in place; march or tiptoe around the room with ribbons or scarves; walk backwards, sideways, or with eyes closed; stretch, including moving arms one at a time across the midline; and games like hopscotch, jump rope, and parachute play (Marchetti 2015).

■ **Practice mindfulness and breathing techniques.** Mindfulness and breathing techniques can help children stay in the present and focus on the now. These exercises can bring awareness to children about their bodies and help them learn to regulate and calm their big feelings. Deep breathing is the simplest strategy to teach young children how to remain calm and to come back to calm (Marchetti 2015). Wherever young children go, their breath is always with them, so it is always a readily available technique. For some young children, simply saying, "Take a deep breath in and then blow your breath out," is not enough to teach them how to calm themselves. Here are some simple games and strategies that can be used during circle time, before eating, and at other times throughout the day to help children focus on the here and now and feel present in the day:

• *Blow out the birthday candles:* Have children hold up both hands in front of them with their fingers spread wide. Explain to them that their fingers are birthday candles on a yummy-smelling cake. Have the children take a deep breath in to smell the delicious cake and then slowly exhale to blow each candle out individually. Do this ten times, smelling the cake and blowing out each candle, until all ten fingers are down.

• *Shoulder-roll breathing:* Have each child choose a comfortable position—on the floor, in a chair, or standing. Ask them to breathe in through their noses, and as they do, have them roll their shoulders up by their ears. Once their shoulders have reached their ears, have them breathe out as they lower their shoulders back down. Repeat this slowly several times, rolling their shoulders up and down in rhythm with their breath.

• *Smell the soup:* Ask each child to cup their hands to create a delicious bowl of soup. To keep the children engaged, they can choose their own kind of soup, or one child can choose the soup for the group. Then tell the children to breathe in the delicious smells of the soup. Model for them how to take a long, slow breath in smelling the imaginary soup. Then explain that their soup is too hot and blow out to cool the soup. Alternate between smelling and cooling the soup several times.

• *Tummy breathing:* Have the children lie on their backs on the floor, and place a small special item (perhaps a beautiful rock or crystal, seashell, beanbag, or stuffed animal) on each of their stomachs. Instruct them to take each breath in deeply through their noses and feel the special item rise and then exhale through their mouths and watch the special item fall. This exercise offers them a chance to practice their breathing as well as practice taking care of something special.

- *Blowing bubbles:* Ask each child to close their eyes (if they feel comfortable) and imagine that they are holding a bubble wand in their hand. Have them take a deep breath in through their nose and let a strong breath out as they blow their bubble wand and watch the bubbles fly around the room. Repeat this exercise several times as the children delight in their imaginary bubbles.

- *The "magic mustache":* The "magic mustache" can help support young children in calming their bodies. The magic mustache is a concept created by Karyn Purvis through her Trust Based Relational Intervention (TBRI) program for children who have experienced abuse and neglect. To help children feel the "magic" and calm their bodies, have them place their index fingers across their "mustache area" and apply pressure, then count to ten. This area is a pressure point that can help relieve stress when pressed.

- *Create calming spaces:* Sometimes children who have experienced trauma can feel overwhelmed by being in a large classroom community, especially when they are having big feelings. We can create safe and comfortable spaces for children to use to calm down from an emotionally heightened state. These calming spaces can be used when a child is wanting some space from the group or needs a quieter area. Sometimes a child may want a teacher to go to the calming area with them to help them calm down, and that is great too! These spaces are never used as punishments, because as we learned in chapter 2 about brain development, disconnecting from children when they are feeling overwhelmed does not help them long term. Any form of isolation, like time-outs, is an ineffective strategy for children who have experienced trauma. Children who are having a hard time regulating need an adult to coregulate with them; cutting them off from connection does not teach them that we will always be available to support them.

Sleep

Children who have experienced trauma frequently have difficulty falling or staying asleep. This can be because they have had scary experiences around nap- and bedtime, but it can also be because their bodies are having a hard time settling down and calming for sleep. This trouble falling asleep can be challenging at naptime in full-day child care settings. There may be an expectation that young children fall asleep on their mats at a specific time every day. However, young children who have experienced trauma may need extra support to make this happen. They may need to be held and rocked to sleep, or they may need to not be touched. Some may need to fall asleep in a room with lights off and blackout curtains over the windows; others may find that too scary and will need to sleep in a well-lit room. Some children will only be able to sleep if they know a caregiver will be sitting next to them when they wake, and some children will be okay waking on their own. Depending on their story and what they have experienced, needs will vary among children. There's no way to know what will feel comfortable and calming for children who have experienced trauma before getting to know them and learning who they are (Burke Harris 2018).

Conclusion

When a child displays specific physical or sensory behaviors on a regular basis, our job as educators is to find out what it is they are expressing through their behavior and find ways to accommodate their needs in safe and acceptable ways. We cannot simply expect children to stop behaviors if we tell them to; we need to support them in finding ways to integrate their bodies and minds to remain calm. A child who is wiggly and constantly moving may seem like they are not paying attention, but they may actually be trying to find ways to stay in the learning zone. This child may need ideas for classroom-appropriate and less-distracting ways to get the movement they need to be able to focus.

Let's take Sabha, for example. Sabha is a kindergartner who loves to jump and is constantly hopping around the classroom, which leads to her bumping into her friends. Her friends respond by yelling at her, which seems to escalate her and leads to more jumping. Sabha's teacher Leticia recognizes that her body needs the experience of jumping, but the way she is doing it is not working for the group. Using some tools from her toolbox, Teacher Leticia integrates jumping into several activities throughout the day. In their morning circle, they play a bunny-hopping game where the children jump from carpet square to carpet square. As they move down the hallway to the library, Teacher Leticia has each child pretend they are an animal, and she gives Sabha the kangaroo. Outside on the playground, Teacher Leticia teaches Sabha and her friends how to hopscotch. At the very end of the day before going home, all of the children stretch out around the classroom to do ten jumping jacks while counting. By integrating these jumping activities into the classroom's daily rhythm, Sabha is getting the physical movement she needs to be successful in the classroom environment.

As trauma-responsive educators, we must be on the lookout for the underlying needs reflected through children's behaviors. We must know that children are doing their best at every moment, and children do well when they can. If a child's behaviors seem to be challenging them or are challenging us in the classroom, we must think of new and alternative ways to help them integrate and calm themselves so they can be successful in the classroom environment.

Chapter 7

Expression of Trauma in the Classroom

Social-Emotional Development

Liam is a five-year-old who was assigned male at birth. For the past two and a half years, Liam has been telling anyone who will listen that she is not a boy but rather a girl and she would like to wear dresses to school. Liam's parents are completely against Liam expressing her gender as she would like and force her to wear khaki pants and polo shirts to school. They have become emotionally abusive to Liam when she mentions her gender, and her dad has hit her when she has asked for dresses or expressed interest in changing her name to Luna. Luna, as she wishes to be called, has gone from being a happy, exuberant toddler to a sad and despondent kindergartner. No one will listen, and every day feels harder and harder for Luna to pretend to be someone she is not.

Yongkang is two years old and has experienced physical abuse at home. At school he has trouble napping, both falling asleep and staying asleep. Recently Yongkang began smearing feces on the wall during naptime. When his teachers notice it happening, Yongkang starts to laugh and runs away.

Perhaps the most significant disruption to a child's development is the impact trauma can have on social-emotional development. Luna and Yongkang are just two examples of young children who have experienced trauma and are now experiencing social-emotional challenges. Early trauma can disrupt several different aspects of social-emotional development, including children's sense of self, regulation skills, perspective taking, curiosity and play, and ability to stay present in the moment when experiencing big feelings. Social-emotional development is foundational for academic learning. To allow children's brains to reach the higher-level thinking that is needed for both complex play and academics, they need a strong sense of self and the ability to interact effectively with others as well as the ability to regulate their emotions.

Social-emotional development occurs through gathering *social-emotional skills*, which include the capacity to recognize and comprehend one's own emotions as they occur, read and understand the feelings of others, regulate and share big feelings in developmentally and socially appropriate ways, and express appropriate empathy for others, as well as the capacity to begin and maintain relationships (National Scientific Council on the Developing Child 2004). Each of these components is crucial because together they create an internal emotional environment that is calm enough to allow for the more complex thinking needed for academic learning. Emotional regulation is an adaptive ability that allows children to engage with those around them in a healthy and beneficial way. Without these skills, children may not be in a calm-enough space to be open and able to learn new academic concepts.

Self-Concept

Children's self-concepts and the impact they believe they have on the world are formed within relationships. As we see with Luna, the way children see themselves is directly connected to how they are treated. Children who experience nurturing and predictable home environments where attachments are strong and physical and emotional needs are met typically develop a positive self-image and view of the world (van der Kolk 2014). This occurs through their caregivers recognizing and responding to their cues: the adults read babies' and children's facial expressions, body language, actions, and noises to identify what they need and what to offer them. When their attachment needs are met and their cues are successfully identified, children learn to develop trust in themselves and in others.

Children continue to turn to their adults to learn about the world throughout early childhood. For example, two-year-old Rosa and her dad are headed to the airport to pick up Rosa's grandma. Rosa spent a little bit of time with her grandma when she was a baby but has not seen her in over a year. When they arrive at the airport, Grandma rushes over and immediately gets down on her knees to talk to Rosa. Rosa moves toward her dad and wraps her arms around his leg. Grandma identifies her cues, takes a step back from Rosa, and begins to talk to both Dad and Rosa about how happy she is to be visiting. Rosa watches her grandma and her dad interact. She sees her dad give her grandma a hug and speak to her in a warm and welcoming voice. Soon Rosa realizes that her dad sees Grandma as safe, and Rosa decides she is ready to try interacting with Grandma again. This time Rosa interrupts Grandma and Dad's conversation to say, "I'm wearing a necklace today." Grandma turns her attention to Rosa, and they begin to reestablish their connection. Rosa is learning by identifying her father's cues what and who is safe. While she is still learning the social skills of how and when to enter conversations, she is well on her way to learning the social-emotional skills she needs to be successful in preschool and elementary school by having appropriate boundaries and appropriate apprehension about new people. Children who develop a positive worldview through foundational secure attachments to their caregivers are typically able to acquire the necessary skills that predict school success. They can stay emotionally regulated and calm enough to adapt to the school's social and academic environment and develop the executive function skills that help them follow directions and stay on task.

However, children who experience early relational adversity may not have an opportunity to experience the consistent serve-and-return relationship, which leaves them without the skills to know how to process their big feelings. The biochemical and structural changes that can occur in their brains can hinder their capacity to recognize, share, and cope with their feelings. To recognize internal emotional states, children must be able to understand what happens in their bodies when they experience distinct forms of arousal and appropriately label that arousal (for example, "sad," "excited," "frustrated"). Children who have experienced trauma may not have the early attachment experiences that help them recognize internal emotional states. Let's take Serenity as an example. Serenity is a four-year-old girl who lives with her mom and infant brother. Serenity's mom is overwhelmed by life as a single parent and is currently experiencing undiagnosed postpartum depression. She spends a lot of time sleeping or watching television and expects Serenity be a "big girl" and occupy herself and the baby when the baby is awake. To pass the time, Serenity's mom sometimes takes her children to the local playground so Serenity can play and she and the baby can sleep in the grass. One day Serenity hears noise coming from across the park and looks up to see a woman and man moving toward the playground, yelling at each other. The man starts hitting the woman, and the woman is trying to fight him off. Serenity is frightened; her heart rate increases, and her breathing becomes shallow. She runs toward her mom and jumps onto her back and holds on tight. Serenity's mom shifts her weight so Serenity slides off and tells her to go play before falling back asleep. Serenity's palpable fear is not acknowledged and no comfort is offered, leaving her feeling alone and confused. The yelling and fighting between the two adults in the typically calm playground alarmed Serenity and caused her to sense danger, yet her mom's dismissive attitude and lack of comfort made her doubt herself. In this moment, Serenity's sense of the world and her mom's response are inconsistent, causing her to second-guess her perceptions of the situation. Serenity is left to work through her fear alone, which leaves her feeling overwhelmed and confused. Serenity's sense of self—how she sees herself in the world—greatly impacts who she is as a learner. If she sees herself as a person who cannot correctly identify social situations and is alone to cope with fears, she may come into the classroom with a lowered sense of self-worth as well as stifled capacities to understand her feelings in different contexts and emotional states.

In chapter 2, I described how children's brain development is influenced by chronic stress. It is easy to see how this early brain development effects self-regulation. As early childhood educators, we must be able to recognize the difference between healthy emerging self-regulation and dysregulation in the children we work with.

In the following sections, I describe what dysregulated behaviors can look like for young children in the classroom. After each section, I discuss some tools and supports that can be offered to children to learn these extremely valuable social-emotional skills so they can find social and academic success in the school environment. To effectively do this, we must be able to critically think about and learn the differences between culturally bound behaviors that we may not be familiar with and dysregulated behaviors that require our support.

Self-Regulation

Foundational to social-emotional development is the ability to regulate. *Self-regulation* is often a misleading term because children learn to self-regulate by coregulating, and coregulation continues into adulthood. Imagine you have a challenging day at work; one child told you he hated you before running out of the classroom, and another student fell on the playground and chipped her front tooth. Not a good day. You come home, exhausted and feeling down. What do you do? Many of us turn to our partners, friends, or family to share our experiences. In doing so, we coregulate. We are calming ourselves and moving through our feelings by sharing them with others. It is as if some of the burden of the day is lifted because it is now shared between you and your confidant. As adults we can often calm ourselves without even having another adult to talk to by processing the feelings ourselves or imagining what another adult would say to help us feel calm again. Young children need an adult to support them in learning these skills. It is through the early attachment relationship that children learn they can have big feelings and process those big feelings. This "serve and return" experience happens over and over again before children learn how to regulate their emotions on their own.

The beginnings of regulation start in utero—the stress, trauma, or depression that an expectant mother experiences can impact a fetus's self-regulatory capacities. If the woman's body is producing stress hormones, those hormones can affect the growing fetus's makeup. For example, studies have shown that higher levels of stress exposure and depression prenatally are related to emotional and behavioral challenges in childhood and stress-related disease in adulthood (Zhang et al. 2018). No matter what, infants have little ability to differentiate between arousal states, and it is only through the consistent and specific responses of their caregivers that they begin to understand and describe their feelings. Children learn through these earliest relationships how to interpret nonverbal emotional cues: when an infant is crying from a wet diaper and the caregiver comes over with an expression of mild worry and changes their diaper, the infant learns that when they are distressed and need something, their caregiver cares about their needs and will also take care of them. However, when caregivers are inconsistent in their responses and behaviors—for instance, caregivers that fluctuate between anger and nurturance in their responses to a wet diaper—children do not learn how to accurately identify and interpret their experiences.

Early inconsistent responses from caregivers can cause children to come into the classroom predisposed to states of hyper- or hypoarousal. They may be constantly on alert because they are unsure what response they will get from the people around them: *Will the teachers be gentle or rough? Will the children play with me or hit me?* Or they may be shut down: *I expect the teacher will be angry with me. I will try to disappear to keep myself safe.* Often because of this difficulty recognizing, expressing, and controlling their emotions, young trauma survivors' expression of emotions in the classroom can be extreme, ranging from heightened and volatile to excessively restrained, blunt, flattened, or dissociative (Child Welfare Information Gateway 2014a; NCTSN 2014).

Children develop the foundational skills for self-regulation during their first five years of life, but for children who experience early trauma, this early skill building may be interrupted or delayed. Current research on trauma reveals that emotional regulation is essential for school success. Self-regulation is foundational for academic learning; people learn best when their bodies and brains are calm (Siegel and Payne Bryson 2011). When children are not able to regulate, their brains are on constant high alert and cannot integrate the new learning that occurs in classrooms. They may have a hard time regulating their big emotions because they lack the impulse control that comes from learning to coregulate with another person. We must first coregulate to learn the skills to self-regulate. Importantly, coregulating is very different than managing children's behaviors. Early childhood educators are so very important in helping children learn these skills; we can be the coregulators for children processing big challenges.

Self-regulation encompasses different developmental domains since it involves thoughts, feelings, and behaviors; children must translate different experiences into usable information that supports them in regulating. As Florez (2011) explains,

> Infants translate the feel of soothing touch and the sound of soft voices into cues that help them develop self-calming skills. Toddlers and preschoolers begin to translate cues from adults, such as "Your turn is next," into regulation that helps them inhibit urges to grab food or toys. They begin to learn how long they must usually wait to be served food or to have a turn playing with a desired toy, which helps them regulate emotional tension.

> Because self-regulation involves different domains, regulation of one domain affects other areas of development. Emotional and cognitive self-regulation are not separate, distinct skills. Rather, thinking affects emotions and emotions affect cognitive development. Children who cannot effectively regulate anxiety or discouragement tend to move away

from, rather than engage in, challenging learning activities. Conversely, when children regulate uncomfortable emotions, they can relax and focus on learning cognitive skills. (47)

Self-regulation is a gradual process, and if children have missed out on learning some of the earliest regulation skills, they cannot simply jump over these skills and join their peers wherever they are. As educators we need to meet children where they are developmentally and offer developmentally appropriate expectations, which is very different than setting expectations based on chronological age. Let's imagine for a moment that you are teaching in a second-grade classroom and working with an eight-year-old child whose self-regulation looks more like that of a four-year-old. How do you respond? Many people would hope that by expecting the same regulatory skills as the other eight-year-olds in the classroom, the child will simply shape up and catch up, but this most likely will not work. Instead it is important to support that child in regulating where they currently are so they may learn the skills needed to catch up to their peers.

Externalizing and Internalizing Behaviors

Children who experience complex trauma in early childhood are likely to struggle with both externalizing and internalizing behaviors. Externalizing behaviors often come from children's suboptimal abilities to plan, organize, and delay gratification. Perhaps you have become exasperated with a student and asked them, "What were you thinking?" Well, that child probably was not thinking; they were more likely impulsively responding to stimuli (Peterson 2014). Here are a few of the *externalizing behaviors* we see in the classroom:

- extreme emotional swings; emotions or behaviors escalating quickly

- aggression toward self and others, both spontaneous and planned; screaming, kicking, hitting, spitting, swearing

- defiance; intentionally opposing or ignoring requests

- irritability and reactivity

- disruptive behavior; silliness or clowning around that severely hinders learning

- saying things that are not based in truth (lying); taking things that do not belong to them (stealing); and finding roundabout ways to get what they need or want (social manipulation)

- big responses and feelings to turn-taking activities, sharing, and games that involve winning and losing

- being easily brought to tears

- challenges in calming and self-soothing

Internalizing behaviors tend to be more difficult for teachers to notice because children are directing their feelings inward and not drawing attention to themselves. Children with internalizing behaviors experience big emotions just like the children who externalize their behaviors; they just keep them bottled up instead of communicating them. For example, three-year-old Scarlett, who has experienced a lot of early attachment disruptions, has been attending a new preschool for about six months. One day she falls on the playground and scrapes her knee. Her teacher sees it happen and notices that it immediately begins to bleed. The teacher walks over to comfort her, and as he gets close, he says, "Ouch! You fell." Scarlett yells "No!" and runs off clutching her knee, wiping away the blood. At first glance, this child may just seem "tough" or "independent," but these are internalizing behaviors; this child is having the same big feelings about getting scared and hurt as other children, but she is not expressing those feelings. She needs help from the adults around her to express her feelings and understand her experiences. Here are some of the behaviors we see in the classroom from children who demonstrate *internalizing behaviors*:

- compulsive compliance with adult requests

- excessive worry or difficulty in changes to routine

- rigidity in toileting and eating requirements

- withdrawal and social isolation

- regression to earlier developmental stages: thumb sucking, toileting accidents, wanting to be fed

- general fearfulness and unwillingness to try new things

- complaints about body aches and pains

- overly controlled need to have specific routines, toys, clothes, and foods

Externalizing behaviors are more likely to be concerning to teachers and caregivers because they are usually big and visible. While children may exhibit different behaviors, manifestations of both externalizing and internalizing responses to emotions can impact the way children see themselves and their learning in the classroom.

Social-Emotional Development: a child's ability to experience, express, and manage emotions and the capacity to form constructive and gratifying connections with others

Self-Regulation: a child's ability to manage thoughts, feelings, and behaviors within a given situation

Externalizing Behaviors: behaviors that are directed toward the external environment

Internalizing Behaviors: behaviors that are directed toward one's self

Social-Emotional Skills and Diagnoses

Although research on brain development, attachment, risk factors, and resiliency measures all indicate that children's social-emotional development is deeply connected to their early experiences, it is becoming more common within the medical field for young children displaying emotional distress and challenging behavior to be given psychiatric labels. These labels are meant to support the understanding of children's mental health but too often are used while overlooking the relationship between their personal experience and their environmental circumstances (van der Kolk 2014). Young children who experience trauma are often diagnosed with alternate mental disorders that encapsulate some of their symptoms without getting to their underlying cause. For example, children who have experienced trauma are more likely to be diagnosed with Attention Deficit Hyperactivity Disorder (ADHD) than their peers. Children diagnosed with ADHD have higher rates of poverty, parental separation, violence, and family drug use than children without this diagnosis (Ruiz 2014; Siegfried and Blackshear 2016). Further, children who have experienced four or more adverse childhood experiences (ACEs) are three times as likely to be taking ADHD medication (Ruiz 2014). A recent report by the Centers for Disease Control and Prevention indicates that between ten thousand and fifteen thousand children ages two and three years old are being prescribed medications for ADHD, such as Ritalin or Adderall. It is much more likely for children living in poverty and receiving Medicaid to be prescribed drugs rather than alternative relationship-based treatments (such as parent-child supports and therapy or early intervention services) (Schwartz 2014; Dell'Antonia 2014). In most cases, the prescription of these stimulant medications and antidepressants for young children is considered "off label," which means they have not been studied on young children and there is no scientific data on the effects of these drugs on children's immediate or long-term behavioral and developmental outcomes. Thus, until studies are conducted on the use and safety of these medications for young children, these children and their developing brains are at risk for unknown and unintended consequences (Schwartz 2014). Not only are the side effects not known, but also the prescription of medication is responding to the behavioral symptoms presented rather than the underlying issue of experiencing trauma (Burke Harris 2018).

To ensure that young children get the support they need, it is imperative to consider their environmental contexts when helping them through mental health issues. Offering young children a responsive and supportive environment is one of the most significant ways to prevent mental health disorders and promote healthy development. Many of the prevalent adult mental health disorders have origins in childhood; intervening in early childhood and creating environments that negate or counteract some of the risk factors experienced by children can change children's mental health trajectories. One important prevention method is to create schools that are aware of and responsive to young children's social-emotional development.

The Teacher's Role: Supporting Social-Emotional Development

The social-emotional challenges we see in the classroom demonstrate that children who experience trauma can become overwhelmed by their big feelings. When dealing with trauma, social-emotional development does not just happen because children get chronologically older; they will not just "mature" out of their behaviors. No matter how their feelings are being displayed, one thing holds true: their behaviors will likely continue until they are offered the support they need to learn alternative ways of recognizing and responding to their feelings.

To successfully support social-emotional development, we need to find ways to teach the important social-emotional skills we hope our children will learn. To do this, we need to identify teachable moments. Often we use the peak of a conflict or emotional event to try to offer skill-building opportunities. However, as we learned in chapter 2, this is often when young children who have experienced trauma are in their stress response, and they are not calm enough to take in any new information. For example, Roscoe and Evan are lined up to wash their hands before snack, and Roscoe tries to move in front of Evan in line. Evan yells, "Hey!" loudly and pushes Roscoe. Roscoe begins to cry. It is usually at this crisis moment (the dotted arrow) that we as educators arrive at the scene and begin to enter into skill building and problem solving with Roscoe and Evan. However, their brains may not be in a calm-enough state to even hear our suggestions, like "Stay in your spot in line" or "Use your words!" To teach both Roscoe and Evan the social-emotional skills they need, we need to catch them pre-crisis (at the circled arrow) to teach them new skills when their brains are

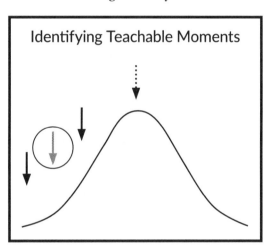

Identifying Teachable Moments

(Joseph et al. 2010)

calm and available to take in new information. Catching teachable moments at the precrisis point takes practice and proactive planning; in this scenario it could happen through preteaching, for the benefit of both Evan and Roscoe, how to form a line, how much space children should give their line buddies ahead and behind them, or offering visual markers to stand on while waiting. Further, knowing the needs of the individual children helps catch soon-to-be crises from happening; if a teacher knows Roscoe has a hard time staying still or Evan has difficulty using his words rather than his body to express his needs, a teacher can stand close to help mitigate the situation before it gets underway. The following sections will offer many suggestions of ways to teach children in the circled arrow, as well as ways to respond to dotted-arrow events (Souers and Hall 2016).

Identifying Feelings, Perspective Taking, and Building Empathy

Taking the perspective of others is an important social and academic task for children to learn. Children who have experienced early trauma may be constantly assessing the mood of their caregiver before deciding how they feel themselves. Let's think back to Serenity, who tried to check in with her mom about the scary fighting she witnessed in the park. She went to her mom to have her fears affirmed and to receive comfort, but she received neither. Repeated situations like this will leave Serenity without a strong sense of self because her feelings are being dismissed and invalidated. Further, children who grow up with emotional and physical abuse may not want to upset their caregivers, so they watch to see what is allowed and when. In doing so, they are losing the opportunity to practice choosing how they feel, what they like, and what they want to do. Without the capacity to fully understand and know themselves, they may have difficulty understanding the wants and needs of others. Trouble taking the perspective of others can cause serious challenges for children in the classroom. These include some of the following:

- difficulty developing and expressing empathy

- lacking the skills to participate in social conversations, where an understanding of others is expected

- problem-solving challenges

- struggling to extrapolate big ideas from texts

Children who struggle with perspective taking are not simply mean or manipulative. To be effective trauma-responsive educators, we need to avoid those labels and support children in developing the skills they require to take others' perspectives.

The Teacher's Role: Supporting Children in Identifying Feelings, Perspective Taking, and Building Empathy

Feelings are at the heart of any internal or relationship-based situation. It's imperative that young children learn *emotional literacy*, which is the ability to recognize, understand, and respond to their own feelings and others' feelings in a socially and culturally appropriate way. This will help children learn the important perspective-taking skills they need to be able to play with peers successfully and problem solve. Emotionally literate classrooms spend time daily discussing feelings and feelings vocabulary. Most importantly, in a classroom where emotional literacy is promoted and supported, feelings are always validated and always okay. Although the big behaviors that may accompany their feelings may not be okay for the classroom and we will need to support children in learning different strategies to express their feelings, all feelings are always okay (Souers and Hall 2016).

Many children do not know how to recognize and name emotions. In the classroom when we are working with children who are having a hard time staying calm, we want to begin to build the basic language and facial cues that go with different emotions. This can be done through *direct teaching* of feelings vocabulary, which involves creating specific activities for children to practice and improve their emotional vocabulary as well as opportunities to learn to recognize how facial expressions can cue us to different emotions. This can also be done through *indirect teaching* of feelings vocabulary, through discussing and naming feelings as they occur. Some strategies for teaching feelings vocabulary include the following:

- **Model how to regulate emotions by discussing your own feelings.** Talk about your own feelings and how you manage them throughout the day. For example, at the snack table, Teacher Shelby is talking to a group of children about their favorite books. Teacher Shelby takes this as an opportunity to teach about emotions. "Did I ever tell you about the time I wrote a book?" she asks. "I was in second grade, just a little bit older than you, and I wrote and illustrated a story. I was so proud of it, and I couldn't wait to show my mom when she picked me up from school. But then an accident happened, and my friend Chloe spilled water on my book! I was very sad. I cried when I saw my soggy book. I sat with my teacher to feel better. Once I felt calm again, Chloe helped me separate and dry the pages, and the book ended up almost as good as new." In this story, Teacher Shelby is offering an example of her own feelings and how she successfully managed them. Through this anecdote, the children can learn that everyone has feelings and everyone has different strategies for moving through their feelings.

- **Notice and identify the feelings of the children in your classroom as they occur.** Label both "good" and "hard" feelings. For example, Teacher Shelby notices two children giggling and smiling together as they look at a picture book. "I am noticing you both are giggling and smiling. You seem very happy to be looking at that book together." A few moments later, Teacher Shelby turns around and sees a child sitting alone crying. "Diego, I see tears coming down your cheeks. You look very sad." By offering them the feelings vocabulary in the moment, we help them connect the physiological responses that occur in their bodies with the language to describe their emotions.

- **Use visuals to support children in recognizing their own feelings.** Children who have experienced early trauma may not be able to connect their internal responses to big feelings with the feeling words themselves. Offering them the language and then visuals they can use to identify big feelings and where they are on a "feeling-o-meter" can help them recognize what big feelings they are having. For example, creating a "mad-o-meter" or "sad-o-meter" can help children identify how big their feelings are.

- **Use visuals to support children in recognizing the emotional cues of others and taking the perspective of others.** Learning facial cues is very important for young children. Children who have experienced early relational trauma may not be able to connect facial expressions with feelings. By offering direct teaching of facial cues, teachers can support children in learning how faces change based on different feelings. This can be done in a multitude of ways. One fun strategy is to make different emotion faces, using the students in your classroom as models. This is a way to build emotion vocabulary while also building community. Whether you use the faces of the children in your classroom or find emotion faces online, once you have them, you can make them into books to post on the walls by each center area or create a "feelings station" with a mirror so children can practice expressing their feelings while looking at themselves.

■ **Use books.** Books are a wonderful and engaging way to teach children about feelings and emotional regulation. Many books that are specifically written about feelings offer a lot of great feelings vocabulary. Talking about the feelings of the characters in the book can bring about good discussions around feelings vocabulary, empathy, and problem solving. Other books offer general feeling themes—"excitement" or "disappointment," for example—and we can offer discussion during or after the read aloud to bring out the underlying feelings expressed in each book. When looking for books for your classroom, it is important to ensure that the characters in the books represent the children in your class. Looking for depictions as well as authors and illustrators of varying races, ethnicities, and cultural backgrounds is one good way to make sure that classroom libraries are culturally relevant and reflective of our children and their experiences.

■ **Play feelings games.** Many games teach feelings vocabulary. Feelings Matching Game is an easy way to bring feelings vocabulary and visual cues into your classroom. Simply create matching feelings cards that young children can view and match. Older children can turn them over and play the game Memory. Feeling Wheel, Feeling Die, and Feeling Jenga are just a few more feeling games. To play these games, spin the spinner, roll the die, or pull a piece from the Jenga puzzle and have the children share an example of a time they experienced the feeling written on the wheel, die, or Jenga piece. For some children, explicitly discussing their own stories about their feelings may be overwhelming, so it is often a good idea to allow a "pass" if they do not have a story to share. Almost any game can become a feelings game with a little bit of ingenuity. Pick-up sticks, for example, can become a feelings game by labeling each stick color as a different feeling: red becomes "mad," green becomes "calm," blue becomes "sad," and so forth.

■ **Make emotion eggs.** Take plain plastic eggs and draw faces on them. Put the eyes and nose on the top half and the mouth on the bottom half. Draw them with different feelings: happy, sad, confused, nervous, surprised, and so forth. Let the children mix and match the tops and bottoms and talk about what feelings the different eggs are expressing.

- **Use songs and fingerplays.** Many songs and fingerplays specifically talk about feelings. You can also take a classroom favorite and turn it into a feelings song or make up your own!

- **Present stories and puppet shows.** Stories and puppet shows are a magical part of the early childhood classroom. Use existing stories that connect directly to feelings, or make up your own stories based on the feelings you are noticing in your classroom. For example, it was the end of the year, and Teacher Gabe noticed that many of the children in his classroom were starting to worry about their move from preschool to kindergarten. Teacher Gabe used what he was noticing in his classroom to write a story about a little fox who was nervous but excited to be moving from his little tree forest school to the big tree forest school where his brother fox attended. Teacher Gabe was able to use storytelling as a way to discuss the fears, worries, and excitement the children were expressing in the classroom. The children were able to identify with Little Fox and connect their own feelings to his. Stories and puppet shows can also be wonderful ways to bring in different cultural values and elements into the classroom. For example, several Jewish fables connect to the idea of doing *mitzvahs*—good deeds—that can teach about the importance of caring for others.

- **Connect cause and effect between actions and feelings.** For many children who have experienced trauma, connecting actions to feelings can be challenging. Imagine Seth, whose father has an alcohol addiction. Seth's father goes through periods of being a loving and supportive father who is attuned to his son's needs and feelings until he starts drinking. Once he drinks his first beer, his mood changes, and he becomes angry and often violent. Seth is not able to understand how sometimes he can make a joke and his dad laughs, and other times the same joke could set his dad off into an emotionally or physically scary tirade. This experience has caused Seth to have difficulty recognizing how actions are connected to feelings. To help children like Seth, we need to work on the relationship between cause and effect. When reading books, stop before turning the page to ask, "How do you think he is going to feel?" Work to link the actions in the book with the feelings that will come.

- **Teach empathy through discussion.** Model empathy with the children. This can be done by expressing empathy when something occurs ("I am so sorry—that sounds frustrating.") or acknowledging empathetic words when someone else says them ("You asked Diego if he was okay, and that made him smile.") Draw children's attention to the feelings of others: "Diego is very sad right now. He is missing his mom. Do you ever miss someone? How do you think we could help Diego?" Focusing on feelings and ways we can support children when they are having big feelings can teach children how to identify with their peers.

- **Teach empathy (and behavior) through role plays.** Role plays can give children the chance to think about how they would respond to another person displaying big feelings or during a conflict. We can ask, "If your friend was crying because he missed his mom, what could you do to help?" Or "How would you feel if you were crying and a friend came over to try to make you feel better?" We can also use role plays to talk about appropriate behavioral responses: "If a friend took a toy you were playing with, what could you say?" This allows children to think through scenarios outside of the moment when emotions can be running high.

- **Use drawing or journaling.** Have children draw or write out their feelings (only if they want to—this should never be a punishment). Make sure to have a safe, secure place for their journals or drawings to go when they are done; they may not want to share their feelings, but they can process them on their own through drawing or writing.

- **Read together, read alone.** Reading a story to children or, for school-aged children, reading a book quietly to themselves, can work as a calming technique. The act of reading activates the logical, regulatory part of the brain, which can help children who are overwhelmed by their feelings.

Challenges in Relationships with Peers and Adults

Because children who have experienced early attachment disruptions or traumas often distrust that others will be predictable, they feel like they need to keep themselves safe. It is a scary and often overwhelming task to be a three-, four-, five-, or six-year-old and to believe it is your responsibility to keep your body and mind safe. This can and often does cause difficulties in relationships with teachers and peers. To keep themselves emotionally and physically protected, they may try to distance themselves from their classmates. They may be distrustful and suspicious of both the teachers and children in their classroom because they are expecting bad things to happen at any moment. Consider Gem, whom I introduced in chapter 4. Gem loves school and loves to learn, but she is having a hard time staying calm when frustrated. Gem lived her first nine months in a world that was unsafe for her, so now Gem is a bright and exuberant three-year-old whose brain is still worried about being hurt. Though she cannot articulate what is happening, her experience is that when she starts to feel close or connected to her teachers or friends, she worries whether they will continue to be safe with her. She feels as though she needs to protect herself to ensure that she is not hurt again. This comes out as big feelings and behaviors that keep everyone distant.

The Teacher's Role: Support Children in Forming Relationships with Peers and Adults

The need for a child who has experienced trauma to distance themselves from their peers or adults in the classroom often looks like big, dysregulated behaviors but can also be calm rejection of affection and closeness. Both responses can be seen as children work to keep themselves safe in a world that feels unpredictable and scary. To support children in building healthy relationships with friends and caregivers, we must first help them feel calm and secure.

We not only want young children to learn how to identify and label feelings, but we also want to give them the skills to effectively regulate their emotional states and to feel open to connection with other children and safe adults. Children are often told to "calm down" without their knowing what calm looks or feels like. We need to offer them ways to calm their bodies and express their feelings. We can create a "toolbox" of strategies with older children that they can choose from, and for younger children, we can create a running list of strategies to offer them. That way they are not trying to reinvent the wheel each time they are upset; they will have some go-to strategies to pull from. Some children will want an actual "toolbox" (this can be a box you decorate together) that has items to use or visual cards describing what to do, and others may just want a printed list. Many of the techniques used to calm children and create soothing and consistent classroom environments support young children's sensory systems. For a comprehensive list of sensory-related strategies (such as mindfulness, breathing techniques, yoga, and so forth), see chapter 6 on physical development.

As you have gathered by now, relationship is the best regulator. Spending extra time to build connections and find common ground with children who are working hard to reject you or push you away can be the best way to change their beliefs about relationships and closeness. To do this, we must observe and be open to knowing each child deeply. Through consistent, open, and loving caretaking, children can slowly learn that you are a warm, safe base for them to return to when things get hard.

Curiosity

Being curious is one of the hallmarks of early childhood. Curiosity allows for exploration of the environment, risk-taking, and trying new things. Children who have healthy attachment relationships with safe and warm caregivers have internal working models that tell them the world is safe and good. When they venture out, they know they have an adult to come back to if something bad happens. They can explore because they have the security of knowing that they are supported emotionally by their trusted adult. While temperament plays a role in this, and as educators we can observe a wide range of ways children demonstrate their curiosity, the underlying theme is one of security and inquisitiveness.

For children who have experienced trauma, their beliefs about who they are may make risk-taking feel emotionally or physically unsafe. Their low self-concept can lead to difficulty exploring and taking risks in the classroom environment. Curiosity is often overshadowed by a desire to be close to their caregivers. Imagine five-year-old Tom, who often wakes to find himself alone in his home. In the classroom, he is very cautious and does not like to try new foods, activities, or even books. His early experiences of being alone when he needed an adult have led him to believe he must care for himself. He does not want to try new things because he may feel frightened or nervous since he cannot trust that emotional support will be there if he gets scared or hurt. As a self-preservation tactic, Tom decides not to pursue new activities. Early trauma can impede young children like Tom from recognizing their personal preferences because they have not had the ability to safely explore and experiment (van der Kolk 2014).

Because children who have experienced relational maltreatment may lack the confidence to explore on their own and try new activities, they may dismiss the activities as boring or stupid. This explanation of why they do not want to try a new activity is often a disguise for their fear that the activity could overwhelm them and then they would be all alone. Children who have experienced neglect may come into a classroom environment and see the other children confidently stringing beads or cutting with scissors—activities that perhaps they have never seen before—and feel overwhelmed, not knowing where to begin and finding it easier to reject the activity rather than show fear or vulnerability.

The Teacher's Role: Supporting Children's Curiosity

Many children who have experienced attachment disruptions or early traumas may be hesitant to try new things and explore new environments, especially loud, boisterous environments such as early childhood classrooms. To support young children who are feeling overwhelmed or shy, try these strategies:

- **Allow time for them to warm up.** We cannot push children to be braver or bolder than they are. We must meet them where they are. To build curiosity, we first need to build attachment. If you have a child who wants nothing more than to sit next to you for most of the day, allow that. Let them learn about who you are and the predictability of the space before pushing them to try new activities.

- **Always notice the shift in their zone of proximal development.** While we should not push children to try new things before they are ready, we should encourage them to try new things when we notice they *are* ready. We must observe children closely to notice when they are ready for encouragement to try something new. Perhaps they have been sitting next to you at the playdough table every morning for a week, refusing to touch the playdough. But today you see them reach their hand toward the bowl and touch the pink goo with one finger. Maybe today will be the day you ask, "Would you like a ball of playdough?" Or maybe today you will not say anything at all and just place a piece of the pink dough on a tray in front of them, available to be touched or not.

- **Stretch curiosity through conversations about things that matter to them.** To build their capacity for curiosity and wonder, we must engage children in conversations about their interests and likes. We can ask questions and demonstrate curiosity and learn alongside them about topics that bring them excitement. Following the children's own interests and ideas is the best way to expand their capacity to think through concepts, ask questions, and hypothesize.

Play

Play for young children typically begins in infancy, when babies explore the environment through objects and people. Babies typically engage in solitary play. Their play primarily involves exploring their environment, fingering different-shaped toys, putting items in their mouths, or placing objects into a basket or box and then taking them out—this is their play. Preschoolers and early elementary-age children continue this type of sensory-focused play when swinging on swings, playing chasing games, and building mud and sandcastles (Hassinger-Das, Hirsh-Pasek, and Michnick Golinkoff 2017). However, children who experience trauma may be so focused on ensuring their environment is safe that they do not feel comfortable freely exploring their environment. When a child is worried that something scary will happen or worried that their caregiver will not comfort them if they get hurt, they may choose not to try new activities or play experiences. Further, as I discussed in chapter 6, some children who experience early trauma may have sensory issues that keep them from feeling comfortable touching different materials.

Children engage in many different types of play. For typically developing children, around eighteen months is the time when children start to incorporate elements of symbolic play into their play experiences. In symbolic play, a child uses objects to stand in for other objects. For example, you may see a toddler grab a banana and place it by her ear to symbolize a phone. Symbolic play is very important for young children's development; it allows children to explore themes and experiences from their own lives. There are several types of symbolic play, including constructive, dramatic, and games with rules.

Constructive play involves building and organizing stackable materials (such as blocks, plastic bricks, and clay) to create symbolic representations of places or objects children know about. In this type of play, children are learning how to envision a structure, plan its creation, and complete the construction (Hassinger-Das, Hirsh-Pasek, and Michnick Golinkoff 2017). This type of play can promote fine-motor development and gross-motor development, as well as further cognitive abilities. However, young children who have experienced trauma may struggle to think through what they want to build and then follow through constructing their vision. This process of completing a multistep activity may cause them to feel frustrated or overwhelmed.

In *dramatic play*, children take on roles of others and use their imaginations to pretend and make believe. Dramatic play allows children the space and time to process what they see and experience in the world in a way that feels comfortable and familiar to them. They can also use this form of play to act out "what if" situations: *What if I was a mama with seven children?* In dramatic play, children often take on the voices and language of those around them, use objects as props in their pretend worlds, and take on a range of different roles. Through dramatic play, children can practice taking on the experiences of another, practice cause and effect, and use their emerging empathy. Often we see young children engaging in *power-themed play,* especially three- and four-year-olds, where the play revolves around having or not having power. In this important play theme, children are grappling with the significant moral archetype roles of "good" and "bad" or "safe" and "unsafe." Children often bring weapons or known superheroes into their power-themed play; even when not offered physical representations of weapons, children will often make or imagine their own. For children who have experienced trauma, their dramatic imaginative play may repeat the scary experiences they have had outside of school. They may get overwhelmed by the feelings that their play brings up, and often their play is more physically aggressive and violent than the play of their peers.

Games with rules allow children to practice playing within a more structured environment. Games with rules can be as simple as Duck, Duck, Goose or as complicated as more-detailed board games. As children play even the simplest of these structured games, they are building their capacity to wait for a turn, follow instructions, and use strategy. Children who struggle with impulse control and turn-taking can struggle during simple games with rules. They may have a hard time cognitively remembering the different aspects of the game and controlling themselves from playing out of turn. Further, games that have a clear winner and loser can be emotionally challenging for children who have experienced trauma. They may have difficulty regulating their feelings of disappointment if they lose, and they may feel like the loss is an indication of their value or worth. For example, Justine is in a pre-K class and loves to play board games. Every day at school, she asks her teachers if they can bring out the board games because she loves the thrill of winning and taking her very own turn. However, Justine hates losing. Whenever Justine loses, which happens often in the chance-based games she plays, she gets very upset and often ends up throwing the pieces across the room and sobbing under the table. Her teachers are beginning to recognize this pattern and are working to find ways to support Justine's social-emotional regulation when she experiences the disappointment of losing.

The Teacher's Role: Supporting Children in Play

In the early childhood education classroom, we typically expect children to be able to play independently—play is the work of childhood, after all! We expect them to explore, to make up games and play scenarios, and to "get to work" on the projects we so carefully create for their enjoyment. However, for children who have experienced relational trauma, playing or creating independently may be an overwhelming task. Often children who have experienced trauma will need guided support from adults during play. They may require more teacher-initiated and direct attention to feel comfortable and safe enough to explore. This means that as the adults supporting the children in feeling safe, we must be aware of the children's interests and help them explore at a pace that feels comfortable to them. Their confidence and curiosity will grow only once the adults around them accept them for who they are and where they are.

Our job is to allow children to feel safe and grounded in their play exploration, while also supporting them in learning new skills. We must not push children far beyond their comfort level into a sink-or-swim type of situation. The zone between what a child is able to do by themselves and what a child is able to do with the support of an adult or more capable peer is what the developmental theorist Lev Vygotsky (1978) termed the "zone of proximal development." The skills that can be developed with adult guidance and peer collaboration exceed the skills that can be attained alone. We must find each child's zone of proximal development and scaffold their learning.

A child who has experienced early trauma may need a lot of time to feel comfortable and safe before you see any movement in their play exploration. To help explain what this might look like in the classroom, I would like to introduce you to three-year-old Leilani. Leilani and her parents lived in a midsize city that just experienced a massive flood, and they were displaced along with twenty-eight thousand other people. Luckily Leilani's mom's sister, Aunt Maria, lived just an hour away and offered to house Leilani and her parents until their house could be rebuilt. This move required Leilani's mom, who has been home with her for the past few years, to get a job so they can try to save the funds not covered by insurance to fix their house. Leilani is living in a new house in a new city and is in full-time child care for the first time. Leilani is missing her old routine and time with her mom, and she is having trouble sleeping and playing alone. She wants to be with her parents every moment she can. At school she sits on the lap of her teacher or very close by as much as her teacher will allow. After a couple of months of Leilani sitting quietly by her teacher's side, she begins narrating the play she sees happening around her: "Jonny and Luke are playing doggies." Leilani is engaging in *onlooker play* as she watches the play of the other children.

Leilani's teacher understands the traumas Leilani has recently experienced, so he is careful to scaffold her learning while not overwhelming her and causing her to shut down. Leilani's teacher uses *parallel talk*, in which he describes what he sees Leilani doing to support her in making cognitive connections between the experience and the language describing the experience. Leilani's teacher says things like, "You are noticing your friends are playing doggies. I see you are smiling; it looks like you are enjoying watching them play." Parallel talk promotes self-regulation, self-confidence, and language development because the language enhances the visual component of learning. Once Leilani is spontaneously sharing her observations, the teacher recognizes it is time to support Leilani's learning by offering an opportunity for growth. He uses language that deepens their connection and reiterates that he is a safe, secure base for her to venture into play from by saying, "Are you a little doggy? You are! Little doggy friend, if you would like to join the other two pups, I can watch you from right here. If you need me, you can come back to me and sit with me again. I always love to have my little doggy friend with me." Eventually Leilani ventures into the doggy play and becomes a third doggy alongside Jonny and Luke. This process, and the relationships that are being built during the process, take months to develop. Leilani's teacher is warm, open, and consistent in his support of her process for months as she uses him as her secure base. She first needs to learn how to feel calm before she can be curious and explore. Our job as educators is to trust that relationships can be built and that it is through these relationships that children can learn to feel safe and curious, which will carry their development and their learning forward.

Dissociation

Dissociation can be a response to complex trauma. As I discussed earlier in this chapter, children who have experienced trauma may be hyperfocused on ensuring their own safety, and in doing so, they may mistake innocuous details as safety threats. Some children dissociate or "go away" in the classroom to protect themselves from these perceived threats. Children may not realize this is happening and may not realize they have missed significant parts of their day.

Dissociation begins as protective in the face of adversity. As Cook and colleagues (2003) explain, although dissociation can be protective, "when trauma is chronic, a child will rely more and more heavily upon dissociation to manage the experience, such that dissociation then leads to difficulties with behavioral management, affect regulation, and self-concept" (14). Dissociation can result in emotional and cognitive confusion; dissociating when feeling overwhelmed by emotions can lead to difficulties in children's identity development because memories can be lost and confused (Cook et al. 2003; van der Kolk 2014). In the classroom, dissociation can be difficult for teachers to identify because the symptoms can be overlooked or confused as "daydreaming."

The Teacher's Role: Supporting Children Who Dissociate

To support young children who experience dissociation in the classroom, we first have to recognize that they are having a trauma response. It is important to then draw on the many strategies described in this chapter and others to help lessen the triggers that cause young children's stress response to activate. See the individualized support plan model in chapter 9 if you are having trouble figuring out what is overwhelming the child and are unsure of which strategies would be best.

Behavior

Disruptions in all development domains influence young children's capacities to manage their behaviors in the classroom. The ability to identify and respond to feelings, regulation skills, and connections to others impact how young children behave and respond in the classroom environment. It is important to use a trauma-responsive lens when responding to children's behaviors in the classroom. However, it is also imperative that we distinguish between trauma-based behaviors and behaviors (or perceptions of behavior) that come from implicit bias and differing cultural norms.

To be effective trauma responsive educators, we must also work to be anti-racist. To do this, we must recognize the harm that schools as institutions have done and continue to do to children of color and their families, and actively reflect on and work towards changing the biases that have caused this harm.

Currently the rates of expulsion for young children attending early childhood education programs are staggering. Nationally, 6.67 preschool-age children attending state-funded early childhood education programs are expelled per 1,000 enrolled; this rate is 3.2 times higher than the expulsion rate for students in public K–12 programs (Gilliam 2005). In child care programs (programs that are not state-funded prekindergartens), the rate jumps to 27.4 expulsions per 1,000 enrolled (Gilliam 2008). More than 10 percent of prekindergarten teachers expel at least one child per year, and of these teachers, nearly 20 percent expel more than one child (Gilliam 2005).

While we know this often occurs because of behaviors in the classroom, research also indicates that these expulsions are not happening at equal rates, and often mental health issues and challenging behaviors are being conflated with racial bias. Specific groups of children are being suspended or expelled, "pushed out" of the early education environment, at higher rates than others. Black preschoolers are 3.6 times as likely to receive a suspension relative to their white peers. Black children make up only 19 percent of children enrolled in preschool, yet they comprise 47 percent of children suspended one or more times (Gilliam et al. 2016). Further, boys are expelled at 4.5 times the rate of girls. Gilliam and colleagues (2016) describe the child most likely to be expelled from a preschool setting using what he calls the three Bs: Big, Black, Boy. Gilliam's latest research noted that despite no behavioral differences, teachers look toward black boys to monitor their behavior and respond as if there is a behavioral problem more often than they do with white boys or girls in general. These staggering disparities are in accordance with research on implicit bias. Therefore, when thinking about challenging behaviors, we must always consider whether the behaviors we see truly are challenging and if there is a trauma response occurring, or if it is our own cultural bias coming into play (Gilliam 2005; Gilliam et al. 2016).

Further, to reduce the extremely high rates of suspensions and expulsion in early childhood settings, we must use strategies that support children in learning how to manage their behaviors, not simply punish their unwanted behavior. The following section will describe some teacher tools that will support children in feeling confident and capable to help them manage and regulate their behavioral responses in the classroom.

The Teacher's Role: Supporting Children in Managing Their Behaviors

The strategies and suggestions listed in this book will go a long way toward calming children which will in turn lessen big behaviors in the classroom. However, some children may still have a hard time staying calm and will need some support in learning how to express their needs and what is using their words instead of their bodies. Below are a few strategies not already discussed that can support children in managing their behaviors.

Avoid behavior charts. Children need to feel safe and connected before their behavior can change. As trauma-sensitive educators, we must focus on relationship-based interventions. We need to offer the foundational skills young children need to learn that they matter and have an impact on the world, which is how they will gain the skills they need to succeed in school. Relationship-based techniques are not quick fixes, although you may see some significant changes right away; they are long-term techniques that take time, patience, and understanding. Often when we are struggling to manage a large group of children, we want quick fixes. Behavior charts are often dangled in front of us as a way to quickly change children's big behaviors, but unfortunately for children who have experienced early relational trauma, they can have the opposite effect.

So what's wrong with behavior charts? This tool comes in many forms, but all revolve around the same idea: encourage positive behaviors and reduce negative behaviors by rewarding what you consider good behaviors and punishing what you deem bad behaviors. Behavior charts typically use colors, stickers, or levels to represent where a child is on the behavior scale. However, for children who experienced early trauma, focusing on the behaviors with positive or negative consequences will do nothing to support them in learning how to recognize their feelings or manage their behaviors. In fact, what it will most likely do is trigger shame for the child and cause even more self-doubt. Children who have experienced an early healthy attachment relationship learn through this early experience that they are good and worthy of good things. They can differentiate between the statements "I did something bad" and "I am bad" or "I did something mean" and "I am mean." When these children with healthy attachments move from blue to yellow on the behavior chart or do not earn a sticker at circle time, their internal voice tells them, *Whoops, I made a mistake and my teacher did not like my behavior. I am still a good person, so I will try again next time.*

But children who did not have this healthy attachment experience may not be able to distinguish between "I did something bad" and "I am bad" or "I did something mean" and "I am mean." When reprimanded by moving down a level or not earning a sticker, these children may be flooded with shame and believe they are a bad or mean child. Rather than their internal voice telling them they made a mistake, their internal voice says, *I am a bad kid. I don't deserve a sticker. I will not be able to change.* Often when children feel deep shame and negativity about themselves, their brains signal the stress response, and the feeling is so overwhelming that their brains believe that more danger is coming, triggering their fight, flight, or freeze response. When this happens, children's behaviors can escalate physically, but they may also laugh or ignore the person who is upset. They can look like they do not care, when actually they care immensely—they are just working extra hard to keep themselves safe. Triggering the stress response is definitely not the way to create a classroom that feels safe. Rather than using behavior charts, we need to focus on the relationship-based interventions offered in this chapter and others to create true healing.

Avoid time-outs. Time-outs are another behavior-related technique that is completely ineffective for children who have experienced trauma. The purpose of a time-out is to send a child to a specific chair or area in the classroom to think about their behavior or to calm down before coming back to the group. However, as we have learned, children learn to regulate their behavior through coregulation. Sending a child off by themselves to think about and change their behavior on their own is unlikely to achieve the results you are hoping for. It may offer a quick break for you from the child's behavior, but it will not create any lasting change in the child's behavior and may create a rift in your relationship. This is why the children being sent to time-out in kindergarten are often the same children being sent to the principal's office in second grade and the same children being pushed out of high school. Time-outs create a divide between you, the adult, and the children who need you the most.

Like behavior charts, time-outs can cause young children to feel shame and internalize the belief that they are bad and unworthy of connection and love. Time-outs send the message to children that your love is conditional and based on behavioral expectations they are truly incapable of sustaining. It is as if you are saying, *I will only love you and want me near me if you behave the way I expect.* Instead we need to send the messages that say, *I will love you and want you near me always, and I will teach you the skills you need to express yourself in a way that feels good to you and to your peers.* Children who have missed out on healthy attachment need consistent connection. They need to know that when they have big emotions and behaviors that make them feel out of control, they have an adult there who can support them through their behaviors. They need to know that they are safe and that connection is always there for them. Psychologically isolating a child causes them to feel more alone in the world than they already do and confirms their already deeply held belief about themselves that they are flawed and unworthy. We need to look beyond children's behaviors to find the need they are expressing. A child who is "sassing you" or "talking back" is actually overwhelmed with fear or frustration and not able to express this in an appropriate way. A child who is kicking or hitting is feeling emotionally overloaded and needs an adult to support them in coregulating back to calm. Sending a child in this dysregulated state to a space by themselves is essentially leaving them heightened and alone. When we think about it that way, time-outs lose their purpose.

Many people will wonder if this just teaches children that their behaviors are okay, and the answer is a simple no. Staying close and connected when a child is experiencing big feelings and behaviors will show them that they are loved, cared for, and supported, which will calm their brains and bodies so they can learn new skills and behaviors. Our relationships with the children we care for are our most powerful assets; it is through connection that we will begin to see change.

Support time-ins. The "time-in" is the inverse of the time-out. Rather than isolating a child in an attempt to correct their behavior, time-ins provide the opportunity for a child's trusted adult to pull them close and help them coregulate. In classroom environments, a "calm-down corner" can be a space that facilitates this process and can be used with the support of a teacher or by a child independently, depending on the child's needs and abilities. This space can be offered to children as a refuge while escalated, though as children learn how to manage big emotions, they may elect on their own to spend time there. Whereas time-out spaces are designed to be devoid of stimulation so children reflect on their behavior free from distraction or activities they might enjoy, time-in spaces contain materials that will help children regulate their emotions: favorite books, breathing balls, stuffed animals to cuddle, or feelings charts. The purpose of a time-in space as opposed to a time-out space is to provide an area where children can calm their bodies and minds in a supportive and nurturing environment.

Keep recess. By elementary school, children are often expected to behave in the classroom if they want to have fun during recess, but as chapter 6 taught us, children whose bodies are overwhelmed need the sensory input that they get during outside play. Much like time-outs, removing children from helpful and healing activities has the opposite effect of what we are hoping for. If a child is successful outside, consider extending recess so children can get more of the good sensory input they need to feel healthy and calm.

State expectations clearly. Often big behaviors come from children simply not knowing what is okay or not okay in a classroom environment. If at home a child solves problems with their siblings by hitting and grabbing, those are the skills they have when they enter the classroom. If we expect them to use different strategies, we need to make this clear. There needs to be clear classroom expectations that all children and teachers can refer to. This also involves making sure that all the educators who work in your classroom are on the same page. Can children talk freely during morning meeting, or are they expected to raise their hands if they have a question? What happens if a child bites a peer? In the hall, does everyone walk together, or do children move down the hallway freely? These may seem like small differences in teaching styles to you and your coworkers, but to children who are living or have lived in chaotic environments, not knowing what to expect from the adults around them can be very overwhelming. In chapter 8, I talk about some whole-classroom strategies to support children who have experienced trauma. Establishing classroom agreements is one important way to create clear expectations for all children in your classroom.

Ignore some behaviors. Just like adults, children sometimes need a little slack. We all make mistakes, and not all of our mistakes need to be mentioned. If some smaller, not-safety-related behaviors are happening, simply ignoring the behavior and moving on may be best.

Make plenty of positive statements. All children thrive on positive reinforcement, and children who have experienced trauma can benefit particularly from affirmation of their goodness and worth. Think about the language you use with children in terms of "deposits" and "withdrawals." Deposits are all the positive reinforcements, verbal and nonverbal, that we give children. Any encouragement, praise, affirmation, acknowledgment, thumbs-up, or high fives paid to children are considered deposits into their emotional piggy banks. "Withdrawals," on the other hand, are any request or expectations we make of children that requires them to spend from their emotional piggy banks. Even when made kindly and with love, a request is still a request. Every time we tell a child to use their walking feet, line up for recess, or pass the milk at lunch, we are making a withdrawal. Withdrawals are not bad, and they are unavoidable. However, we can lessen the toll that withdrawals take on children by making enough deposits to ensure that their emotional piggy bank balances stay in the black. Setting a goal to give children five deposits for every one withdrawal keeps us mindful that the majority of our interactions with the children are positive and affirming. By following the 5:1 ratio, we ensure that children have emotional currency to spare as we make the requests necessary of them to be successful in classrooms.

Use puppets. Puppets can be used during whole-class activities and also with small groups of children to practice problem solving and managing big feelings. Puppets are a great way to address challenging classroom behaviors right away, without calling attention to a particular child or situation.

Offer redos. Children who have experienced early traumas may come into the classroom without the skills to appropriately handle social situations and problem solving at school. To support them in replacing their maladaptive behaviors, we need to offer strategies they can use and opportunities to try out the more prosocial and effective strategies. One example might be, "Nadia, please do not push José off the bike. If you would like a turn, please ask, 'May I have a turn?'" By offering a behavioral replacement, we are giving them the skills they need to successfully change their behavior next time. As discussed in chapter 2, children's brains are making new neural connections all the time, and with practice and repetition, their brains will catch on to the new language and appropriate ways of interacting in the classroom. Please do not get discouraged if the process seems slow; it can take a long time to see the progress, but it is happening!

Repair relationships. To be trauma-responsive educators, we must have the tools to rebuild and repair relationships with children when things get hard. Since we now know children will learn and develop through relationship, we need to always work to rebuild fractured relationships with children after they have expressed challenging behavior. To do this, once the child is calm and ready to talk about what happened, we can begin teaching the child skills they need to repair the relationship. We can talk about what happened in a non-blaming way and plan for what will happen next time. Making a plan after an incident offers some good practice for future planning and lets the child know that they are believed in.

Resolve conflicts. Many children do not come into school with the skills to share their feelings and needs, hear the feelings and needs of others, and problem solve. We must offer children the specific language they can use to get their needs met: "Billy, you can say, 'Can I have a turn?'" offers Billy the useable information he needs to begin the sharing process rather than simply saying, "Ask nicely!" or "Kids, remember to share!"

Set clear limits. Adults can support children in feeling safe in the classroom by having clear and consistent limits about safety. If a child's behavior is feeling out of control, we do not want to simply try redo after redo; we want to change the environment and set limits around behavior. It may be as simple as saying, "Nadia, it looks like the bikes are not working for you right now. Let's choose a different area to play in. Would you like to go to the sandbox or go blow bubbles?" Limits and consequences should never be punitive; they should always be directly connected to the behavior that was being displayed, and the point is to be helpful to the child's development, not simply upset them. If Nadia is pushing children off the bikes and cannot calm her body enough to behave differently, she may need to move to a different space on the playground for a bit to help recenter herself. This is not punitive; it is not done to shame her or to make her feel bad, but to help her brain have positive experiences at school.

Conclusion

Supporting young children's social-emotional development is one of the most important roles of early childhood educators. It is only once children feel emotionally safe and calm that academic learning can really take off. Through consistent, loving, and healing practices, we can help children learn to recognize and respond to their big feelings in the classroom. In doing this, we can work to create classroom environments that support confident and competent children who feel calm and loved.

Chapter 8

Whole-Classroom Strategies

CHILDREN HAVE THE CAPACITY TO EXPRESS JOY, excitement, and love for their friends, families, and schools, even after experiencing unimaginable pain and hardship. As trauma-responsive educators, we must see the good in children. We must recognize each child as valuable and worthy of love and respect. Our job is to delight and find wonder in their accomplishments, no matter how small. It is important that we always look to support areas where children may need growth within the context of the things they do well. If we cannot find joy and amazement in who they are, how can we possibly expect them to feel that way about themselves?

When children's development is altered due to early experiences, it can lead to behavioral challenges as well as mental health diagnoses that attempt to encapsulate the developmental outcomes of traumatic experiences. Too often children do not have the support of adults who understand their experiences, which leads to children being labeled as mean, manipulative, liars, or thieves, rather than recognized as trauma survivors struggling to make sense of the world. Sometimes this misunderstanding of what trauma looks and sounds like in the classroom can lead to well-intentioned teachers and counselors spending years working within behavioral modification frameworks that are not conducive to change in children who have experienced trauma. To reach all children, we must create trauma-responsive classrooms that are focused on building relationships and adapting the curriculum and environment to individual needs. Trauma-responsive educators must believe that children do well when they can, and our job as the adults in schools is to figure out the strategies and tools that work for the children in our classrooms.

All children share the same inherent desires for safety, love, and connection; behaviors that counter these needs are adaptive strategies that come from children attempting to fulfill their unmet needs. To change the strategies they are using, we need to meet their needs; we need to lean into rather than away from them when behaviors get big or hard. By using relationship as the foundation of everything we do with young children who have experienced trauma, we are working to repair the hurt and pain that came before us and to offer a different perspective for ongoing hurt and pain. As the previous chapters have described, there are many strategies that can support the different developmental domains. In this chapter, I discuss some of the whole-classroom and environmental strategies that can be used to create an atmosphere that supports healing.

Classroom Strategies to Support All Learners

To create trauma-responsive spaces, we must build relationships between the adults and the children and between the children themselves. Trauma-responsive classrooms are built through creating a sense of safety, empowerment, trust, and connection. Children need to feel safe and connected before they can be calm enough to learn new behaviors or skills. We must focus our energy on relationship-based interventions rather than behavior-modification techniques, because we are working to change children's sense of self and their understanding of the impact they have on the world. Relational strategies are not quick fixes, although you may see some significant changes right away; rather, they are long-term techniques that take time, patience, and understanding. By engaging in consistent, healthy, and responsive relationships, we are offering children a new way of seeing the world and themselves.

Classroom Strategies to Create Safety

Trauma-responsive classroom communities are built on mutual respect, cooperation, trust, shared power, and a sense of belonging. A truly trauma-responsive environment is both culturally responsive and constructive; the children must see themselves in the space and know that their voices and ideas matter (Souers and Hall 2016). Here are some strategies to create a sense of safety in the classroom. Most of these are whole-group strategies that are beneficial for all children and vital for children who have experienced trauma.

Find and acknowledge strengths. As adults we can support children in learning that the classroom environment is safe by first meeting them where they are. An important piece of this is recognizing their strengths. We must see and acknowledge what they do well to be able to find effective strategies to support their growth. It is easy to get caught up in the challenges children are experiencing and the challenges we have caring for them, and we can forget to see the highly adaptive and often extremely creative behaviors the children demonstrate. To notice strengths, we must ask ourselves, *What does this child do well? Where and how do they connect to their peers? To their teachers? To the classroom environment? Which children or adults do they seem drawn to? What areas of the classroom do they love to explore? How does this child inspire me? What is loved about this child?* By noticing what children do well, we can find ways to build on their strengths. We are practicing the love and empathy we want to show them as they develop and are opening our minds to see them as whole people beyond their differences or delays.

Use culturally responsive practices. To support all children in the classroom, but especially children who have experienced trauma, it is vitally important that our classrooms are culturally responsive and aware. The children we work with need to be represented in our classrooms so they can build a sense of belonging. We must communicate to them through both our words and our environments that they are visible and that they matter.

To support children who have experienced trauma in the classroom, we need to deeply know our children and their families and the different expectations they may have in their homes and communities. We must also be aware of the broader social, economic, and political context we live in and how this shapes the lives and opportunities of the children and families in our schools. We must recognize that many communities, specifically communities of color, have had negative experiences with "helping systems," such as the criminal justice system, child protective services, mental and physical health care systems, and schools. This can influence the ways families interact with teachers and administrators and the roles they take in their children's schooling. Even when we come from the same racial, ethnic, or cultural group as the majority of the children and families we work with, we must think about how our position as educators influences how families see us and their trust or mistrust of our roles. How will your families who live in overly policed neighborhoods respond to and experience a dress-up corner that has been transformed into a police station complete with police uniforms and stuffed police dogs?

We must be continually learning about and discussing how historical traumas currently influence systemic racism in our country to support young children who have experienced trauma. We must work to recognize our own cultural lens and biases and to see how our personal experiences shape our expectations for behavior, our interactions with children, and our views about what learning looks and sounds like in the classroom. While recognizing the influence of historical trauma, we must be careful not to generalize about groups of people. We must let the children and families we work with define themselves and their experiences.

Educators who successfully support young children who have experienced trauma see children within their social context and work with community resources to best support each child. Teachers must understand children's social contexts and connect to the individual children, their families, and community supports available to the families. Rather than focusing on the individual pathology of the child, teachers must consider and try to combat the role societal issues such as prejudice, stereotyping, familial socioeconomic resources, and employment or educational opportunities have on young children and their development. We must support the children through supporting the whole family. With this kind of inclusive model, we are less likely to misdiagnose children as having a mental health problem due to cultural misunderstanding, because teachers and families are working in partnership. We are also more likely to be able to effectively serve children whose behaviors are connected to trauma histories.

As trauma responsive and culturally responsive educators, we must believe that the ultimate goal is not to achieve compliance or control in the classroom but rather to offer all children equitable opportunities for learning.

Create a classroom culture based on mutual respect and belonging. Only once we are culturally aware and responsive can we begin to truly build a classroom culture based on mutual respect and belonging. We must see the children in our classroom as valuable and capable and people we can learn from.

Offer a clear and consistent daily rhythm. We can support children in feeling safe by creating a consistent and clear daily rhythm. Through consistency children learn what to expect each day at school, which can temper some of their hypervigilance and their focus on keeping their bodies and minds safe. By maintaining a clear daily rhythm, children also learn that their big behaviors or emotions will not overpower or change the day's activities, which is helpful for setting boundaries and demonstrating to them that they are safe and the teachers are there to hold boundaries for them.

If there are changes to the rhythm, children may need lots of warning before it happens, support during the change, and discussion after it happens to process it. As I discussed in chapter 4, they may not have the cognitive skills to put what happened in sequential order or the capacity to remember all the details, but we can help them remember their experiences by discussing them.

Offer clear and consistent expectations. The parenting program Circle of Security, which supports attachment between children and their caregivers, describes that to best support children, the adult must be bigger, stronger, wiser, and kind. Children feel safe when they are not in charge of everything that happens in their lives. It feels safe to have adults holding developmentally appropriate boundaries and ensuring that these boundaries do not move. To support young children's sense of safety in the classroom, we must deeply know each child and consider how best to be bigger, stronger, wiser, and kind for them. This can lessen children's hypervigilance and expand their capacities for curiosity and play.

Maintain an unhurried pace. Moving quickly and frantically from space to space can feel overwhelming for any child, especially a child who has experienced trauma. We must move calmly and slowly through our day so the children's bodies can remain calm and slow as well.

Provide flexibility within consistency. Trauma-responsive environments must be flexible while also maintaining consistency. Within the structure of the day, teachers must be able to respond to the interests, needs, and experiences of the children in their classrooms. Reflecting on the daily and weekly rhythms of the classroom and making changes to better support all children when necessary is essential.

Be mindful of transitions. For many children who have experienced trauma, transitions can be challenging. Children who have experienced abuse and neglect have often experienced multiple losses; they may have lost their attachment figures, homes, siblings, friends, toys, clothes, and more. While transitioning from one activity to another may not seem like a huge deal to us as adults, for children who have experienced early loss, it can feel like another loss. They must give up something they are enjoying to gain something unknown. This can cause anxiety and big behaviors during transitions.

Further, as I talked about in chapter 4, children who have experienced trauma can often be rigid in their thinking and actions. This inflexible thinking can make transitions challenging; children may want to stay where they are and continue the activity they have been working on to minimize chaos and maximize their sense of power and safety.

To support children who have experienced trauma in learning to manage their feelings during transitions, we can use a few different strategies:

- **Find ways to reduce transitions.** Often in the early childhood education classroom, much of our day is spent transitioning from activity to activity. To lessen the stress that can come from transitions, lessen the number of transitions in your schedule. To do this, write down your daily rhythm and reduce and combine activities as much as possible until longer chunks of time are available for unhurried activities and transitions.

- **Teach the expectations of transitions.** We cannot assume children understand how and why a transition is taking place. Early in the year, or whenever we notice a child is struggling, we need to proactively teach what the expectations are during the transition. This can occur through modeling, role plays, and using visual cues to support the transition. Take, for example, Teacher Marquis. He is teaching a new group of three- and four-year-old children and wants to start his year off right. For many of the children in his class, this is their first time in school. He noticed that the first few days of school, he was the only one cleaning during cleanup time, and he wants to set the children up for success for this daily transition throughout the entire school year. During his morning circle time, he brings out pictures of the messy classroom, a child cleaning the classroom, and the clean classroom to show his class. He talks about how to clean up, and then he asks a few children to role-play cleaning up with him. He makes it silly and practices throwing toys in baskets and hiding dress-up clothes under the rug until the children, all laughing, tell him he is doing it wrong. "What should I do differently?" he asks, and one by one several children describe how to clean up. A few children volunteer to model how to clean up toys in the right way, and all of the other children watch. At the end of their discussion, Teacher Marquis uses Velcro to post the pictures of cleanup time on the wall next to their poster describing their daily rhythm. The children can see the visual cues, and Teacher Marquis can take them down and bring them over to children who need a little more help during cleanup.

- **Use similar phrases or songs during transitions to create rhythm and ritual.** Sing the same song or few songs as you move from your classroom to the gym, or ring the same chime as you ask children to gather for circle.

- **Make transitions fun.** There are many wonderful songs, poems, fingerplays, and games that can be used to make transitions enjoyable. For example, ask children to come to the line to go outside as if they are moving through honey or as if they are tiny mice scurrying away from a hungry cat, quickly and quietly. Or instead of all the children rushing to the cubbies to put their coats and boots on at the same time before going outside, play an I Spy game to transition children to the cubbies one or two at a time: "I spy someone wearing a blue-and-white striped shirt" or "I spy two people wearing jeans." Once the children guess themselves or a friend guesses them, the spied person gets up to get ready. This can lessen the noise and movement during transitions, which can help children remain calm during what could be a more stressful time.

- **Keep transitions short.** With quick transitions, children are more likely to feel successful and proud to make it through to the next enjoyable activity.

- **Stay close and offer guidance.** If you know you have a child or children who struggle with transitions, get close and on their level to offer them support before, during, and after the transition. Give them warnings that the transition is going to occur: "In five minutes, it will be time to clean up for circle time. Is there a last thing you want to do before it is cleanup time?" For some children, a hand on their shoulder or eye contact can offer different sensory modalities for connection and support. For other children, touch or eye contact may be overwhelming, so it is important to know the individual children well to respond to their differing needs.

- **Be an external regulator.** For some children, transitions are just too much and too challenging to do alone. If this is the case, a teacher may need to stay with a specific child throughout the transition and model and coach them through each step in the process. By being their external regulator and supporting them through the transitions, they are learning that transitions can go well and they can feel safe as they transition. This closeness is setting them up for independence when they are ready.

- ■ **Allow for transitional objects.** For some children, taking an object with them from activity to activity can be very comforting. Stuffed animals, blankies, or special toys can lessen the anxiety about moving from one space to another and can help them feel safe and protected.

Maintain unconditional positive regard for all children. All children need, want, and are capable of love and connection. We must believe this to be true and respect children as individuals who are doing their very best. It is their behaviors that are challenging, not the children themselves. To create trauma-responsive classroom environments, we must understand how the behaviors and trauma symptoms we are seeing are adaptive behaviors that children have learned to keep themselves safe. If we are focused on being angry or frustrated at the children themselves, we are missing out on understanding what they are communicating to us through their behaviors and symptoms.

Working with children who have experienced trauma can be overwhelming and can quickly affect our feelings for and the way we interact with a child. To best support children in our classrooms who have experienced trauma, we must always hold positive regard for the children themselves. We must recognize that their behavior often challenges the children themselves, as well as the adults and other children in the classroom. By viewing the behavior as challenging rather than the child, we can teach children the social-emotional skills to change their behavior and teach the other children how to respond to behaviors they do not like and advocate for their needs (see chapter 7).

Be nurturing and aware of children's personal needs and stories. Traumas cover a wide range of experiences, and as sensitive educators, we must be aware of the differing needs and triggers of the children in our care to avoid retraumatizing them. Some children may greatly benefit from hugs and touch, but for other children, this may be overwhelming and triggering. When we are struggling to understand children's triggers or specific needs, we can conduct observations and create individualized support plans, discussed in chapter 9.

Classroom Strategies to Support Empowerment

Children need to feel competent and have some ownership over their own lives. As trauma-responsive educators, we are called to support children in feeling empowered in the classroom. We want them to know that their voices matter and that we care about who they are individually. To support children in knowing that who they are matters, we need to create proactive, rather than reactive, classroom environments that focus on building children's sense of empowerment. Here are a few ways to help children learn and feel that they are capable:

Offer choices. Many children who live in overly controlled and traumatic home environments may not have a lot of opportunities to express their wants, needs, and interests. They may not have opportunities to share power or to show that their opinions matter. To support children in learning that the world can be safe and predictable, we need to create classroom environments that are built on mutual respect and belonging. One way to do this is to share power in the classroom and allow for children's voices.

In the classroom, we can support children's learning how to identify what they want and need by offering them lots of opportunities for choices, which helps them feel like they have some control over their lives. In doing so, we are also avoiding power struggles where we are demanding something specific and a child is refusing to comply. Instead we are working with the child to find a solution to the problem that meets both of our needs. When offering choices, it is important to remember that even the smallest choice can feel big to a child who has not had the experience of choosing anything before. All young children need developmentally appropriate choices, so we are not going to offer "grown-up" choices like asking one child to decide if the entire class goes out for recess or stays in to play board games. Instead we offer small, manageable choices, such as "Your socks got wet outside. Would you like to borrow red socks or blue socks?" This offers children the opportunity to make choices without overwhelming them and making them feel like they do not have someone holding the boundaries around them.

Offering Choices

Step One:

Take a moment to pinpoint what it is you want the child to do. Ask yourself, *Is this really a choice? Does it show understanding of the child's point of view? Does it show respect for the needs of the situation?* If it is truly an authentic, positive choice, continue on to step two!

Step Two:

State clearly to the child, "You have a choice." This should be said without judgment or anger, because remember, this should not be a power struggle. We only offer choices when there is truly a choice.

Step Three:

State two positive choices that support the child in successfully completing the task. Before offering the choices, make sure both choices are authentic and doable. Say to the child, "You can choose _____ or you can choose _____."

Step Four:

Ask the child which of the two authentic positive choices they want to pick. Say to the child, "What do you choose?" Offer a moment for the child to think and respond. If the child does not respond, you may want to state the choices again or use visual cues to help communicate the choices.

Step Five:

Reflect back to the child the choice that was made. Say to the child, "You chose _____!" in a loving and supportive voice.

Acknowledging That the Child May Want Something Else

"I know (or see or understand) that you _____ *and* we still need to _____. Would you like to _____ or _____? You can decide.

Example: "I know that you really want to continue building your block tower *and* we still need to clean up for lunch. Would you like to clean up the wooden blocks first or the colorful blocks? You can decide."

Tell children what they *can* do. When children are having a hard time regulating and remaining calm in the classroom, it is easy to get stuck in the "no" rut: "No hitting!" "No talking during circle!" "No more roughhousing!" But often children need explicit descriptions of what they *can* do instead. When a child has not learned an alternative to hitting to express frustration, they have no skills to turn to in order to effectively change their behavior. We need to explain to children how they can share their feelings in a prosocial way. For example, you can say, "If you are wanting a turn with the truck, you can say, 'Can I have a turn?'" This gives children tools to use in the moment and more tools to use next time when they have other big feelings.

Encourage leadership. Helping children feel empowered and take on leadership roles can counteract some of the helplessness that can occur from experiencing traumatic stress. By exploring books, themes, and movements where individuals or communities had to overcome hardships or fight for privileges, we can encourage the children we work with to stand up in a positive way for what they believe in. By giving children leadership roles and demonstrating that we value their insight and beliefs, we can be seen as their allies instead of their adversaries.

Create a proactive classroom environment. To support children who have experienced trauma, we must create proactive rather than reactive classrooms. We must work to teach the important social-emotional skills they need to be successful in the social and academic contexts of school. See chapter 7 for concrete strategies to support social-emotional development.

Allow for play. Play is one of the most important aspects of young children's lives. It is through play that young children can create, explore, adapt, experiment, communicate, socialize, and master new skills. Play is fun, joyful, imaginative, and freely chosen. Children understand the world around them and build and extend their knowledge and skills through play. Children often work through conflicts, make sense of their experiences, and explore different feelings and roles via play themes. As the trauma experts Richard Gaskill and Bruce Perry (2014) explain, play is "an essential experiential element of social, emotional, physical, intellectual, and psychological development. The somatosensory experiences in some play activities have been viewed as the neurological foundations for later advanced mental skills, such as creativity, abstract thought, prosocial behavior, and expressive language" (180). Play allows children to construct knowledge and make meaning of the world around them. Through play children learn to thoughtfully plan, problem solve, compromise, take risks, self-regulate, and begin to have a deeper understanding of their own lives and the lives of others (Hassinger-Das, Hirsh-Pasek, and Michnick Golinkoff 2017).

For children who have experienced trauma, play may not be the relaxing and pleasurable activity it is for their peers. Children who have experienced adversity may not be able to comfortably explore because the play itself can trigger overwhelming feelings that can hinder their abilities to regulate, assert themselves, and solve conflicts. Living with overactive stress responses can cause a constant state of stress, which counters the sense of well-being that comes from play. Children who have experienced trauma may bring the stress they experience into their play, making their play into games that revolve around winning or losing, control, conflict, or aggression. Further, they may replay their traumas in play and get stuck reliving the traumatic experience (Child Welfare Information Gateway 2014a). When children's lives are full of chaos and unpredictable behavior, that is what they know, so that is what they bring into their play. They will need adults to anchor their play for them and model healthy, enjoyable play activities. Teachers can support children in expanding their play by offering a myriad of play experiences, such as costumes and props that support different play scenarios, as well as support when play goes awry. If we see that a child is struggling in play, either solitary or coactive, we can be there to help them expand their imaginative options as well as problem solve and negotiate with their peers.

Hold high expectations. It is important that we hold all the children in our classrooms to high expectations while being aware of individual children's developmental needs. We can offer choices and scaffold their growth and development while also ensuring they are participating fully in our classroom communities. If we believe in them, they will learn to believe in themselves.

Classroom Strategies to Establish Trust

Children need to learn that adults can and should be trustworthy. As trauma-responsive educators, we can do this by offering safe, consistent, and responsive classroom environments. We want young children who have experienced trauma to learn that we are true to our word, take responsibility when we make mistakes, and care about who they are as individuals. Here are a few strategies that can build trust between educators and students:

Always work on connection. To show children who have had unpredictable or inconsistent early lives that our classrooms are different, we must always work on connection rather than focusing on correction. Use morning arrival, naptime, and meals as times to build relationships. Greet children as they enter in the morning, ask them questions about the evening before or their morning before coming to school, and use this time to connect with the children's families. Allowing slow and authentic transitions can help families feel welcomed into the classroom community. During meals sit down with children and eat with them. Talk to them about their day at school and the food they are eating. Demonstrate to the children that meals are times where connection and communication occur. When we take time to connect to children throughout the daily routine, the children will learn to trust in the routine and our consistency throughout the day.

Use nonjudgmental language and ask questions. We can use nonjudgmental language to explore why children are expressing big feelings or behaviors. Trauma-responsive educators avoid using language like "You're being sneaky" and instead use neutral language such as "I see you are leaving the table with Jennifer's cookie!" We can be curious about their intentions and ask questions as a way to learn more about their fears, needs, and wants, which in turn will help us create proactive classrooms.

Follow through. If you tell a student you are going to do something, make sure to do it if at all possible. Children who have experienced trauma are often used to disappointment and adults going back on promises. To establish trust, we must always try to follow through with the commitments or promises we make. If you cannot for whatever reason, check in and share why you had to go back on your promise.

Avoid assumptions. Make sure to ask questions and investigate before drawing conclusions. Often a child's intentions or expectations for how a scenario will play out will be different than we originally expect.

Apologize when you make mistakes. We all make mistakes; we may forget to follow through with a promise or make decisions that upon further reflection do not align with our values. When these types of errors occur in the classroom, it is okay to take responsibility for the mistake and apologize. Young children can learn through our example that mistakes can and do happen, and what's most important is how we repair and move on from our mistakes.

Classroom Strategies to Connect with Others

A defining characteristic of early childhood education programs that success-fully support young children who have experienced trauma is that they under-stand children's social contexts; they are connected to the individual children, their families, other educators, and the community supports available to fam-ilies. Within this kind of inclusive model, children are seen and supported in every area of their lives.

Connect with families. To best support young children, we need to connect with their families. Our children's families are our partners and our best allies, and we must strive to build rapport and connection with them. To build authen-tic and true connections, we need to value and believe in them as caregivers to their children. Children's grown-ups love them, whether they have made mis-takes in the past or not, and judging or shaming them for past choices can be counterproductive. We need to support them in being their best selves. Every-one deserves love and compassion.

Families who have experienced intergenerational trauma may associate school with shame and failure, based on the harm schools have done to them in the past. We must acknowledge and work to repair these past traumas through offering different experiences and demonstrating commitment and care for our families.

Nicola is a young mother who has a strained relationship with her parents. When she was eighteen, she got a job at a local convenience store and moved into a small studio apartment. She quickly started a relationship with Danny, her store manager, and got pregnant almost immediately, something that was not in her plan. Danny convinced her to keep the baby, and for several months, they had a loving and supportive relationship. However, once their baby, Danny Jr., arrived, Danny's behavior started to change; he went out a lot in the evenings and was not helping with the baby at all. Nicola began to complain about his absences, and that is when the domestic violence began. Nicola, now a mom at nineteen with no dependable family, felt all alone and decided it was best to stay with Danny until one night when Danny Jr. was two years old. Danny came home late at night, drunk, and nearly put Nicola in the hospital. Nicola packed her and Danny Jr.'s bags and found a nearby domestic violence shelter. After a few months of living in the shelter, Nicola found a new job and another studio apartment and has put Danny Jr. in full-time child care so she can work. Nicola is worried about Danny Jr. being away from her for so long, especially since his challenging behaviors have escalated ever since they left his dad, but she does not feel like she has any other choice. Luckily Danny Jr.'s teachers are committed to finding ways to communicate with Nicola and support Danny Jr. in their classroom. Through their early talks about the best ways to communicate with Nicola, they learned that she always has her phone on her, so they began to send her texts and photos throughout the day to share Danny Jr.'s successes in the classroom, showing how he made pizza and ice cream out of playdough, tried black beans for the first time at lunch, and offered his friend a hug after she fell on the playground. And when things are hard, they briefly share in the classroom face-to-face at the end of the day what they are working on to support Danny Jr. Through sharing all that is going well, as well as their strategies to support Danny Jr. when things are hard, they build up trust with Nicola, who confides in them late on a Friday afternoon what happened with Danny Jr.'s father, her concerns about Danny Jr.'s behavior at home and at school, and her struggles to keep the lights on at home, even while working full-time. Together Nicola and the teachers make a plan to support Danny Jr. across environments. They come up with language and strategies to use when his emotions overwhelm him, and his teachers help Nicola find the resources she needs for a low-income grant to lower her electricity bill. Danny Jr.'s teachers have empathy for Nicola but never pity, so she feels heard, validated, and supported rather than inadequate. Slowly, very slowly, over the next several months, Danny Jr.'s behavior begins to stabilize. Nicola shares with his teachers successes he has at home, and they continue to share his successes at school. Nicola feels like her whole family is being supported at Danny Jr.'s school, and when Danny Jr. eventually goes to kindergarten, she enters his elementary school with the expectation and understanding that she will be a valued partner in his school life, a belief and understanding that will help Danny Jr. flourish in elementary school and beyond.

Just as Nicola's experiences shows, the research on family involvement demonstrates that children are more successful in early childhood education programs if their families feel supported and included in the daily happenings of the classroom. Family involvement is a significant and important element in supporting children's social-emotional and academic success in early childhood education classrooms as well as their academic success in the following years (Caspe, Lopez, and Hanebutt 2019). Therefore ensuring that collaborative relationships and positive communication is happening in our classrooms is an important part of supporting children who have experienced trauma.

To support families and to form lasting healthy relationships, we can use the following strategies:

- be warm and friendly

- recognize families' cultures, communities, and lived experiences as important and valuable

- offer frequent, open, and honest communication

- acknowledge the importance and difficulties of parenting

- validate their ideas and points of view

- speak to families with curiosity and without judgment

- celebrate the children and sharing good stories as well as the challenging things you are working on in the classroom

To be trauma-responsive educators, we need to partner and work with the children's families. Familial participation is one way to promote healthy and collaborative relationships between teachers and families. Many different practices and strategies can be used to enhance family participation. Here are a few:

- daily check-ins at drop-off and pickup with families

- family-teacher conferences

- inviting families to visit the classroom

- inviting families to help with classroom activities and outings

- Family Discussion Nights where families get to participate in discussion around one topic (such as how to handle power struggles or ways to support literacy at home)

- a class newsletter

- email, telephone, and text communication

- printing photos, sending home artwork, and writing down interesting stories and anecdotes from the children

- providing written and oral information about the program's philosophy, policies, and expectations

Family involvement in the classroom is associated with children's improved development and academic skills (Caspe, Lopez, and Hanebutt 2019). Children who have experienced trauma need all of the adults in their lives to be in communication, and as educators we can foster this through our daily commitment to connection.

Connect with colleagues and other professionals. When Nicola came to Danny Jr.'s teachers with her worries and concerns, they were not simply about Danny Jr.'s behavior—her worries extended into how to keep Danny Jr.'s life safe and stable as she worked a minimum-wage job as a single parent. Luckily Danny Jr.'s teachers were connected to other professionals who were able to give them resources they could pass along to Nicola, which in turn increased Danny Jr.'s stability and success in the classroom. To best support children in the classroom, we must collaborate with other professionals who have expertise in fields connected to early childhood education.

- **Other educators and administrators:** When we are stuck or have challenges, we must ask for support from colleagues. We can bounce ideas off others and learn through their experiences. Our colleagues may have different techniques or ideas they have used with other children that can be beneficial for us to try. No matter how long we have been working with children who have experienced trauma, we always have more to learn and new strategies to try. Sometimes an outsider can look at the situation with a fresh perspective and come up with a strategy that we may have overlooked.

- **Physical therapists:** In schools, physical therapists (PTs) use specific body-related interventions to support children's development and help them learn to move, restore mobility, reduce pain, and promote wellness and age-appropriate participation in the classroom. PTs use their understanding and skills specifically connected to motor and self-care abilities to support children's authentic participation in the classroom. Here are a few of the things PTs can help children learn to do:

  - crawl so they can move from place to place, get their toys, or follow their teachers around the classroom

  - learn to sit so they can build the core strength they need to play on the floor with their friends, learn to stand, and eventually walk

- improve balance so they can walk on uneven ground such as sand or grass

- ride a bicycle so they can ride around the playground with their friends

- hold, explore, and play with different toys or objects so they can build, create, or participate in self-care activities

- develop coordination so they can run, climb, slide, and jump

- PTs can support children who have experienced trauma with motor delays, balance issues, and adaptive abilities, all of which can help children stay in their learning zones more often at school.

■ **Occupational therapists:** Occupational therapists (OTs) help children with developmental delays and sensory-processing issues learn to perform and manage day-to-day activities. OTs can also help with feeding issues, sensory overload, dressing, toileting, and other daily living skills. OTs can work with teachers to modify the environment, activities, and routine so children can fully participate. To understand what this looks like, consider Bennett, a two-and-a-half-year-old with an extensive trauma history. He was born with both methamphetamines and heroin in his system and spent two weeks in the Neonatal Intensive Care Unit in withdrawal before moving to a temporary foster home for three months. At this point, his cousin learned he was in foster care, and he moved again to be with family. His cousin was not expecting to parent a baby and works full-time to support her family, so Bennett immediately entered full-time child care, where he has consistently been for the past two years. Around eighteen months, Bennett's teachers noticed that he seemed to get very overwhelmed whenever the classroom got loud, especially when the teachers would sing or play music. When the music would start, he seemed to get listless with a blank, shocked look on his face, and sometimes he would even drool. Bennett's teachers were wondering whether his response was sensory related or if he was simply so overwhelmed that his body shut down from the stress. They tried different techniques to support him (offering a two-minute warning before the music came on, having him sit on a teacher's lap, asking him if he would like to take a break during the songs, and so forth), but nothing worked.

Luckily Bennett qualified for early intervention services and had regular contact with an OT. His teachers reached out to the OT and asked for ways to support him during music time, and her suggestion was transformative for Bennett and his comfort in the classroom. She suggested that as the singing or music started, Bennett's teacher take his hands and clap them together a few times before letting them rest again. She described how Bennett's body was feeling overwhelmed, and a little reminder that he could still move his body could be all he needed to feel in control again. Bennett's teachers were concerned that touching and moving his body when he was already clearly overwhelmed would be more triggering, but the OT urged his teachers to try, so they did, and it worked. After a few claps, his teacher would put his hands back down, and he soon began clapping on his own. He looked more engaged during music time and stopped drooling. As he grew, he continued to seek out a teacher as a support at the beginning of new movement songs and games. For example, if the class sang a song or played a game that involved jumping, he would seek out an adult to hold his hands the first few times he jumped before running off to jump on his own. This seemed to be his way of grounding himself and reminding himself that he was in a safe environment and that he had someone to turn to if he needed support. Bennett's experience is just one of the many different strategies OTs can offer to support children who are having challenges with daily living skills and sensory issues.

- **Speech pathologists:** Speech pathologists, like PTs and OTs, are specialists who can work with children with developmental differences. Speech pathologists typically work with children with both expressive and receptive communication needs. They also work with children with oral-motor coordination issues, such as chewing and swallowing, as well as articulation, auditory processing, and communication-related social skills.

- **Mental health professionals:** Early childhood education environments that have access to mental health or behavioral consultation are less likely to expel children from their programs than those without any access to or knowledge of mental health resources (Dwyer et al. 2012). Having access to mental health professionals in early childhood programs allows teachers, families, and other professionals to work together to identify and respond to the children's needs, organize and implement classroom interventions, and help families develop coping strategies to use in their homes. Children, families, and teachers can all benefit from the reduced stress and enhanced resilience that can come from specific mental health support.

Find outside resources. To be effective trauma-responsive educators, we must be constantly seeking out new research, techniques, and ideas to support children who have experienced trauma. This can happen through reading books and articles, watching videos or webinars, and attending conferences. A few of the prominent resources for working with children who have experienced trauma are the National Child Traumatic Stress Network, the Trauma and Learning Policy Initiative, and the Trauma Center at JRI.

The Classroom Environment

The physical environment sets the stage for how children will feel in the classroom. A messy, chaotic space with little distinction between play areas will feel very different and elicit different responses from children than a well-organized and thoughtfully laid-out space (Bernheimer 2019). Creating a nurturing and well-planned environment is an important component of creating trauma-responsive classrooms. Here are some trauma-informed design strategies to think about when planning the classroom environment.

   Spaces that are culturally sensitive and relevant. As noted earlier, it is vital that our classroom spaces reflect the children and families we serve. We must use authentic books, toys, and other items that reflect who our children are and the communities they come from. It is very important that we use a critical, social-justice lens when we look at the items we choose to place in our early childhood environments. We must ask ourselves who the space is designed for and who will feel comfortable in the space.

   Spaces that are thoughtfully designed. When designing our classroom spaces, we must be thinking about what we want to communicate through our space and how we hope our students will use the different classroom areas. Are certain areas for quiet activities or for big-movement games? Can some areas get messy while others should stay rather clean? All of this can and should be communicated to the children by the design and layout of the classroom space.

Spaces that are well organized and free of clutter. Disorganization and clutter can be overwhelming for all children, especially children who have experienced trauma. When your life feels chaotic, having a highly organized space can create a sense of safety and calming.

Spaces with pleasant smells. Have you ever walked into a room and all of a sudden had an overwhelming memory from childhood? That is because our sense of smell is closely linked to memory. In our classrooms, we want to be mindful of the smells to ensure that children are not being triggered by avoidable smells. Further, we can create healthy new smell associations by offering pleasant smells in our classrooms.

Spaces that do not overload the senses. Often early childhood education classrooms are full of bright colors, bulletin boards with busy borders, and colorful posters. While it is important to create an environment that appeals to the children, we also want to make sure we are not overloading their senses when they enter the space. Choosing calm colors and keeping the space simple will allow children to focus on connection with each other and with the teachers.

Spaces that invite exploration and creativity. To support the children's healthy exploration, we can make sure that our curriculum and environment change based on the children's interests and development. Setting up invitations for tower building or painting before the children arrive will help them enter the space ready to explore.

Spaces with different sensory and tactile elements. Children want to explore using all of their senses. Including different sensory experiences into your daily routine will offer children who need more or less sensory input a chance to find calming materials.

Spaces that reflect the children and families through photos and pictures. To create a classroom environment that supports safety and community, we must commit to valuing and including families in the space. Finding ways to learn about children's important adults and family members allows for more connection and a deeper level of understanding.

Spaces for gross-motor play. Children need to move! Ensure your space has ample room for gross-motor play, both inside and outside, and encourage big-body movement.

Spaces for quiet and calm. Children need to rest! Some children will want to calm themselves through quiet space and time alone or with one or two other people. By creating a designated space in your classroom for children to go to find that calm, children can learn to regulate their own needs.

Indoor plants and outside environments with natural elements. Connection to the natural world is deeply important for healthy development. Have easy-to-care-for plants inside, and create outside environments that bring in elements of nature and allow for nature exploration. Twigs, rocks, seeds, leaves, sand, dirt, water, and more can all be used to build a healthy and caring relationship with the environment.

Self-Care

We need to feel calm, strong, and supported if we want to be trauma responsive. We must care for ourselves so we are available to care for others. To care for ourselves, we must be self-reflective and continually thinking about how our beliefs and ideas shape our responses to children. Working with children who have experienced trauma can feel overwhelming and can trigger one's own experiences of trauma from the past. Those who work closely with children who have experienced trauma may be at risk for "vicarious trauma" or "compassion fatigue," which refers to the impact of sustained connection to those who are experiencing trauma symptoms. Self-care is vitally important to stave off compassion fatigue and to remain emotionally available and calm with the children in our classrooms. Here are a few self-care tips that can help you stay calm and emotionally available to the children you work with:

- **Get enough sleep.** Most people need at least eight hours of sleep per night to feel effectively rested. Getting to bed early so several hours of sleep occur before midnight can also improve sleep and feelings of restfulness in the morning (Marchetti 2015).

- **Take a warm bath.** Bathing in water hotter than your body temperature can help calm you. Spend ten minutes or more semireclined in the water. This position allows the kidneys to move off the adrenal glands, which changes the release of the hormone cortisol, which is connected to stress (Marchetti 2015).

- **Exercise.** Just as physical movement can help young children remain calm, exercise can help us feel calm and energized for our work. Find ways to incorporate at least fifteen minutes of physical movement in your day.

- **Know your limits.** When you are overwhelmed in the moment or in general, take a break. Ask a colleague to step in for you so you can have some time to collect yourself and regroup. There is no shame in needing to take some time for yourself, and that is the way you demonstrate how to remain emotionally stable and healthy to the children in your care.

- **Seek out assistance.** If added support is needed to remain calm and focused, find that support through colleagues, friends, family members, or paid professionals such as therapists. Therapy should never be seen as a sign of weakness but rather one of strength and growth. Being in relationship with anyone, especially young children who have experienced trauma, is hard work, and sometimes we need the support of others to help us through.

- **Find ways to reflect.** To care for ourselves, we must understand how our own identities and worldviews shape our work with young children. Our capacity to manage the stressors that can occur in the classroom will expand as we reflect on who we are and how our position in the classroom influences children and their behaviors.

Self-care is different for everyone, and the suggestions above are just a few of the ways to center and balance yourself so you are emotionally ready and available for the children in your care. We each have to figure out what works for us. Whether that's meditation, cooking nice meals, attending family gatherings, or seeing a movie with friends, we must each hold ourselves accountable to doing it so we do not burn out. Our community's children need educators who care about creating trauma-responsive environments.

Conclusion

Guiding a classroom of young children is no easy task. By using trauma-responsive strategies and techniques, we can build classroom environments that are supportive and inclusive. Through collaboration we can humbly acknowledge that we need support just as the children in our classrooms need support.

Chapter 9

Individualized Support

As we have seen, trauma can influence children's development in unique ways. As educators we may need to adapt our classrooms and modes of teaching to meet their needs. Sometimes, even after changes.

For example, a child who pushes when they want a toy may not have the words to ask for a turn. Or another child who clings to a teacher all day may not trust that the adult will be there for them if they go off to explore in the classroom. Once we understand what children are telling us through their bodies and words, we can use our relationship-based interventions to nurture the children's strengths and offer reparative experiences to counter their pain. In this chapter, I discuss how to use our knowledge of trauma and its impact on young children's brains and development to create individualized support plans (ISPs) as a way to recognize and accurately interpret what young children are communicating through their behaviors.

Individualized Support Plans

Individualized support plans can support children in learning new ways of being and interacting in the classroom. Not all children who have experienced trauma will need an ISP to help them thrive in the classroom, and not all children who benefit from an ISP have experienced trauma. ISPs can be beneficial for many different needs, but they can be particularly helpful when we are trying to determine the triggers and most sensitive responses to children's trauma. While ISPs often discuss the delays or behaviors we see in the classroom, their purpose is really to understand the messages children are communicating through their behaviors so we can hear and respond to their needs. *What are their bodies telling us about how their brains are responding to what is happening?* Through this process, the children will learn via relationship-building activities and skill-building strategies feel differently in the classroom (Fulton and Macrossan 2008).

When trauma-response behaviors hinder a child's experience in the classroom, they can be deemed challenging or baffling behaviors. While some challenging or baffling behaviors are developmentally typical and subside with responsive guidance, some challenging behaviors persist across time. When working with children who have experienced trauma, it is important for us to be able to parse which behaviors are developmentally typical and which behaviors need more support. We can define *challenging* or *baffling behavior* as any atypical repetitious behavior that hinders or is at risk of hindering young children's prosocial interactions or academic learning. These behaviors include but are not limited to persistent emotional outbursts, physical violence, verbal aggression, vocal outbursts (such as screaming), destruction of property, self-harming, consistently not adhering to requests made by adults, and social withdrawal. Although we are focusing on pointing out the behaviors, we are doing this primarily to be able to find ways to strengthen the relationship between teachers and children and to home in on some of the skills children need to be successful in the classroom environment.

Children's expressions of their traumas can take different forms and are greatly influenced by the ways in which we respond to the child in the moment, as well as the child's home life, the classroom environment, the child's disability, and/or the child's developmental stage. The impact of these behaviors in the classroom can be tremendous. The child's trauma-response may result in the following:

- challenging the children themselves, as their bodies feel out of control, and their education or development is interrupted

- challenging the other children as they try to make sense of the behaviors they are witnessing and experiencing

- challenging the teachers as they try to make sense of the children's trauma-response behaviors as well as continue to teach the whole class

Therefore when children express trauma symptoms in the classroom, it is important for teachers to be prepared to respond sensitively and appropriately. As discussed in previous chapters of this book, there are many trauma-responsive techniques we can use to support children's cognitive, language, physical, and social-emotional development. Sometimes when the behaviors continue to persist even while we are using our known trauma-responsive tools, taking a closer look at children's behaviors as a means of understanding what is happening in their bodies and brains can help us create a plan of action to support them in feeling calmer.

As trauma-responsive educators, we know that children who have experienced trauma are not simply trying to be "bad," "misbehave," or "manipulate"; they are working to keep themselves safe in the only ways they know how. Children do well when they can, and if they are expressing behaviors in the classroom that are counterproductive, our role is to figure out how to build relationships with them and change the classroom in ways that allow them to do well. If children's development and behaviors are being consistently affected by their trauma histories, and our general trauma-responsive classroom strategies do not seem to be influencing what we see in the classroom, it may be time to write up an ISP. ISPs involve a process of observation, documentation, assessment, and planning to understand and address children's trauma symptoms and to support children in developing cognitively, linguistically, physically, socially, emotionally, and academically in the least-restrictive early education environment. All children want to feel accepted, safe and loved—ISPs can help us help them get there.

The Individualized Support Plan Team

Creating an ISP is a collaborative process that values the input of the child and the important adults in the child's life. The ISP team can include teachers, family members, directors or principals, school social workers or counselors, speech pathologists, occupational therapists, physical therapists, pastors, community elders, and others. An ISP does not take the place of a child's early intervention or special education documents, such as an individualized family service plan (IFSP) or individualized education program (IEP), but rather it can incorporate elements of these documents to make direct actionable goals that can be implemented in the classroom. By the time an ISP is done, teachers will have a better understanding of who the child is within their social context as well as their trauma triggers and the ways to respond to their trauma response behaviors in the classroom.

There are many different ways to create and implement ISPs. The structure outlined in this chapter is offered as a loose guide to follow as you incorporate the many different tools and strategies offered in your school and classroom context. Creating an ISP includes many valuable steps; this is a long process that can take several weeks or more to create and implement. To create a successful individualized support plan, the ISP team must complete the following:

1. Learn about the child's history, outside diagnoses, and presenting issues.

2. Look for patterns and examine and interpret findings.

3. Create a written plan that offers consistent, relationship-based interventions.

4. Reflect on and make changes to the written plan as a team.

By step 3 in this process, the ISP team has created a living document that can be read, agreed upon, and modified as the ISP is initiated and continually reflected on (Fulton and Macrossan 2008).

Figure 9.1. Individualized Support Plan

Child's Name: _____

Write the child's name here.

Classroom: _____

Classroom name and/or ages of students in the classroom

Teachers: _____

Names of the child's teachers

Date: _____

Date the individualized support plan is written

Report Written By: _____

Name(s) of the person(s) writing the ISP

History Relevant to Current Behaviors:

Include social history, family history, previous medications, relevant prenatal and/or perinatal events, and developmental and academic history as appropriate and relevant.

Outside Diagnoses:

Record any outside diagnoses or current referrals in place that the child has. Examples include failure to thrive (FTT), language disorder, attention deficit hyperactivity disorder (ADHD), oppositional defiant disorder (ODD), etc.

Current Behaviors:

Include the child's strengths as well as responses to the experienced trauma.

Strengths:

Area(s) to offer more focused support:

> **Support Plan:**
>
> *Write the strategies that will be used to assist the child in feeling safe, accepted, and calm.*
>
> ---
>
> **Support Plan Revision:**
>
> *Write the ways the support plan changes (if it changes) at the ISP reflection meetings every three to four weeks.*

Adapted in part from Fulton and Macrossan 2008.

The following sections describe each step of the ISP process in detail.

Step One: Learn about the Child's History, Outside Diagnoses, and Presenting Issues

The first step in the process of developing an ISP is to gather information as we can about the child's history, current diagnoses, and areas for growth we see in the classroom.

Gather History Relevant to Current Behaviors and Outside Diagnoses

As I discussed in chapter 2, children's brain development is greatly impacted by their earliest experiences, so the more we understand the children's histories, the more we can support them in the moment. It is important to remember as we gather this information that sometimes confidentiality and ethical guidelines will exclude us from obtaining some information about children. Often as classroom teachers, it is not pertinent or ethical for us to know all of the details about children's backgrounds.

For example, let's learn about Josh, a three-year-old preschooler who is struggling during mealtimes. Josh's mom experienced severe mental health issues, but she truly was trying her best to be a good parent. She exclusively breastfed Josh up until the age of two and did not realize he was not receiving enough milk or nutrients. Josh often ate cat food out of the cat's bowl on the ground or rummaged through the garbage to eat coffee grounds or old bits of food as a means of filling himself up. At twenty-seven months, when he was removed from his home and placed into foster care, he weighed only eighteen pounds. These are horrific details about Josh's past that probably cause each of us to have a strong visceral reaction; we want to protect Josh and make sure nothing like this happens to him again. This information may feel like it is necessary for us to feel emotionally invested in supporting Josh so he can learn that he will always have enough food to eat at school. However, it is probably not necessary for us to know that much information. Knowing that Josh experienced food insecurity up until twenty-seven months will probably be enough information for us to support him successfully in the classroom environment. Knowing the details of Josh's food insecurity does not actually give us any more useable information about the best ways to work with him in the classroom. We must be careful not to overstep our role and position as educators to feed our own curiosities. Some of the relevant information we may want to gather includes the following:

- the child's family background

- the child's racial, cultural, and religious identities

- the child's past and current living situations

- important people in the child's life

- significant events the child witnessed and/or experienced

- past and current health issues and medications

- activities the child participates in outside of school

- the child's past experiences in a group setting

- the child's interactions with children and adults in different settings

- records of developmental screens or intake forms

- any current diagnoses or referrals in place

Observe and Record Current Behavior

Once we understand the child's background and have written it into our ISP form, we can start to document the child's strengths and trauma-response behaviors or developmental gaps we are seeing that are leading us to develop the ISP. Here are some of the pertinent questions we can ask to help us understand what is going on for children:

Strengths

- Where is the child most successful in the classroom?

- When is the child calm and engaged?

- Where do we see the child feeling competent and confident?

- What motivates the child?

- Which teachers does the child naturally gravitate toward?

- Which children does the child seek out in play?

- What do we love about the child?

Areas to Offer More Focused Support

- What are the trauma responses or patterns we are currently seeing in the classroom that are causing us to want to develop an ISP?

- What strategies calm the child most effectively?

- Are there any noticeable triggers and warning signs that the child's stress response is taking over?

By documenting strengths before delving into areas where growth is needed, we can hold in the forefront of our minds a view of the child based on the fundamental truth that children are loving and deserve love, rather than simply focusing on challenging or baffling behaviors. Using this approach, we can remember and recount all of the ways the child is successful in the classroom and, importantly, what we adore about the child. This reminds us, as an ISP team, to celebrate the child for what they bring to the classroom and school community. From a strengths-based perspective, we get to focus on building relationships and partnerships with the child and their family that highlight successes and help the child feel accepted and calm. For the child, building on strengths will allow for more successful social interactions and group participation. For the child's family, this experience of the ISP team focusing on strengths can be a reminder that their child is loved and adored, no matter their needs (Fulton and Macrossan 2008).

It is only once the strengths are documented and celebrated that we begin to try to figure out the patterns that may explain why children get triggered or overwhelmed throughout the day. Specific times of day or situations can be particularly stressful for children, and being aware of these times so we can support children successfully can be helpful:

- transitions: from home to school, between activities, teacher changes (for example, breaks), and from school to home

- circle time or group meetings

- mealtimes

- direct guidance situations

- moments where there is a high level of noise or lots of children in a small space

- playtime: challenges including, negotiating play roles, and so forth

- when other children bump, hit, kick, or bite

- when there are substitute teachers and other unexpected occurrences

Moments of transition, unexpected events, and relationship struggles can cause any child to feel frustrated or overwhelmed. However, children who have been exposed to trauma may be more affected than expected and have a harder time bouncing back from a stressful experience. Rather than expecting them to simply get used to the change, we can find ways to support them through these more difficult moments.

ABC Functional Assessment Cards

To understand the specific situations that influence children's feelings and behaviors, we must gather information through objective observations of the child and their environment. Children do well when they can, we know that our classroom environment and the strategies we choose to use influence the children's internal states and their resulting external behaviors. Documentation is essential in understanding and working with children who have experienced trauma because it can help us understand relational and environmental issues that influence the children's sense of safety and security in the classroom. Observations are most helpful when the observer has a comprehensive understanding of early childhood development. No matter what observation method or tool a classroom or school chooses to use, what is most important is that the tools are used to understand the child's underlying needs and internal states. We use these tools to find ways to build a sense of safety, security, and confidence in young children who have experienced trauma.

The first step to understanding how to support young children who are displaying challenging or baffling behaviors is to work to recognize their underlying needs; we can do this by gathering data about what is happening for the children currently in the classroom. Sometimes if there is one challenging or baffling behavior, we can simply focus on that behavior—such as biting—and then document the context around the bites that happen in the classroom. However, often for children who have been exposed to trauma, the behaviors we are trying to understand are multiple and varied and connect to their foundational sense of self and their internal working models. In this case, recording the different behaviors we see can help us find similarities between behaviors and create strategies for that specific cluster of underlying needs.

To begin to understand children's internal states and ways we can better support them in the classroom, we can use ABC Functional Assessment cards and/or other classroom or school-approved observation tools (Chazin and Ledford 2016). One helpful element of the ABC cards is that they allow us to gather data about what happens *before* a child is stressed and displays a challenging or baffling behavior, what occurs *during* the incident, and what happens *after* the incident. Through this process, we can work to figure out what the function of the behavior is. What is the child trying to tell us through this behavior? What is the child's body telling us about what is happening in the child's brain? What is the child's underlying need?

Here is a visual of the ABC Functional Assessment Card, adapted in part from ConnectABILITY.ca:

Figure 9.2. ABC Functional Assessment Card

Date and Time:	Child's Name:	Observer's Name:

DEFINITION OF BEHAVIOR:

Describe what you are seeing (if you can), e.g., biting, running from the classroom, or social withdrawal.

GENERAL CONTEXT:

This box is used to describe the general context of the incident you are recording:

- *Where did the experience occur? (e.g., classroom, playground, hallway)*

- *What was happening when the experience occurred? (e.g., children were washing their hands, taking off their shoes)*

- *Who else was involved in the incident or nearby when the incident occurred? (e.g., friend, teacher, family member)*

- *What materials were involved in the incident? (e.g., a doll, food, a jacket)*

ANTECEDENT:

What happened before? Document what was happening directly before the experience.

- *Where was the child?*

- *What was the child doing?*

- *What children or adults were present?*

- *What were the other children or adults doing?*

BEHAVIOR:

What happened during the incident? Using objective language, write what occurred during the incident:

- *If there was a context change: Where did the behavior occur?*

- *What did the child being observed do?*

- *Who else was involved? What did they do?*

- *How long did the incident last?*

CONSEQUENCE:

What followed the experience?

Record what happened right after the incident. The word consequence *can be misleading—this is not simply about what consequence was imposed (although it may be that); rather, it is about recording whatever occurs after the incident.*

- *How did the incident resolve?*

- *What reaction did the teachers, other children, or the observed child have?*

- *What happened after the incident was over?*

Circle the underlying need demonstrated by what you observed:

If possible, make your "best guess" (your subjective opinion) about the function or purpose of the behavioral strategy used by the child. What is the underlying need being expressed?

*Are they trying to **escape** or **avoid**: Attention? An object or activity? Sensory stimulation? Power? Something else?*

or

*Are they trying to **gain**: Attention? An object or activity? Sensory stimulation? Power? Something else?*

To conduct these observations, we must attempt to describe exactly what we see and hear in a precise way, recognizing that our personal experiences and subjective sense of the world will always interfere with true objectivity. However, we can try to be as objective as possible by writing down what we see directly, leaving out any subjective interpretations or biased language. Here are examples of two observations of Josh (who, as mentioned, has experienced food insecurity during his first two years of life) that record the same event. The observation on the left is written as objectively as possible, and the observation on the right is written in a subjective way that plainly demonstrates the educator's bias:

Figure 9.3.

Objective Observation	Subjective Observation
Sitting at a snack table with three other children, Josh leaned forward and took the community bowl of strawberries into his hands and moved it close to his body. In a louder voice than he had been previously using, he said, "These are mine—you can't have them!" Looking up from her seat at the table, Teacher Mara said, "Josh, those strawberries are for every-one. Please put them back into the middle of the table." Josh looked over at Mara and then spat into the bowl of strawberries.	Sitting at a snack table with three other children, Josh noticed that there was only one bowl of straw-berries and selfishly grabbed the entire thing for himself. He rudely yelled, "These are mine—you can't have them!" Teacher Mara was right there at the table and knew they were for everyone, so she said, "Josh, those strawberries are for everyone. Please put them back into the middle of the table." But Josh was impulsive and mean and spat into the bowl of strawberries to ruin snack for everyone.

To gather enough data points to figure out the underlying needs of a child so we can meet those needs, have several (at least five or six) ABC Functional Assessment cards completed before trying to analyze the observations. Each time an incident occurs, write down your observations—some will be missed, but try to gather as many as you can.

When filling out the ABC Functional Assessment Card, make sure to fill in all the descriptive information, including the child's name, the context of the incident, the observer, and the date and time. Each of these different elements can give some clues to the child's underlying needs. Perhaps after analyzing several ABC Functional Assessment cards, you will notice that all the incidents occur ten to fifteen minutes before snack, which can indicate that the child is hungry. Or perhaps they only happen in the loud building area of the classroom, which can indicate that noise or sudden movement is a factor. Each of these sections will give clues about what the child needs to feel safe and be successful.

The most important sections are the ABCs. The first section, the Antecedent, is what happens before the incident. So, for example, in our experience with Josh and his strawberry spitting, we can describe what happened before the incident: "A bowl of strawberries and a bowl of crackers were placed on each of the four snack tables. Josh was the second student to wash his hands and chose a table with no other children. As three other children joined the table, he was heard talking louder and louder, saying, 'I want to eat strawberries!' three times. Teacher Mara heard Josh and went to sit by him to try to help him regulate his volume." This gives some of the context that can help with analyzing the data later. Did Josh sit at a table without other children for a reason? Was he worried there would not be enough? Did the one community bowl confuse him because he assumed each child would receive their own bowl? These questions can help interpret Josh's behavior and find solutions that can help him learn that there will be enough food for him at every meal.

The second section of the ABCs, the Behavior, records the challenging or baffling incident that we want to analyze as a means of finding ways to understand the underlying needs of the child. For Josh, the behavior involves his taking and spitting in the community bowl of strawberries. After this section is written, the Consequence section describes what happens after the primary incident. This does not mean you must describe an actual consequence that was imposed on the child; rather, it describes what happened after the incident. For example, after Josh spat on the strawberries, "Teacher Mara said loudly, 'Oh no! Now your friends cannot eat those strawberries.' Sarah, who was also sitting at the table, said, 'Josh, you're disgusting,' and Veda said, 'Josh, I wanted to eat strawberries!' and began to cry. Josh smiled and said, 'Now I get to eat all of the strawberries.' Teacher Mara responded, 'You may not sit at the table if you are spitting. Please go to the rug until the other children are done with their crackers.' Josh began screaming, 'No, I'm hungry!' and stood up and threw his chair. He tried to hit Teacher Mara, and Teacher Mara yelled, 'Stop it!' which seemed to startle Josh. He moved to the book corner, where he cried 'I'm hungry!' until the end of snack."

Knowing Josh's background with food insecurity and this one incident give us a lot of information. With this information alone we can begin to think about better ways to respond to Josh. If our goal is to bring Josh a sense of felt safety and security, denying him food will not get us there. We can begin to change our classroom practices immediately, while continuing to gather more observations and data. Once we have five to six incidents concerning Josh's responses to meals and eating time in the classroom, we will be able to analyze and interpret the information to help figure out how better to support Josh's relationship with food and his relationship with his teachers and peers.

Step Two: Examine and Interpret Findings to Look for Patterns

Once we have completed our observations of the children and the environmental factors influencing their feelings and behavioral expressions in the classroom, we examine and interpret the recorded observations and concerns. We will look for patterns that affect the children's experiences at school; we will look for patterns in the days of the week, times of day, or specific people or events that influence the child's level of stress, sense of safety, and needs. Sometimes the act of observing, documenting, and adapting to what the child's behavior is telling us will resolve the initial concern, and we will not need to continue with our analysis. Or we may immediately see a trigger or cause for the behavior and an easy-to-implement solution. However, if we still have concerns, we must work to create an ISP that can support the whole child in their development.

These are questions to ask when analyzing the observations:

When?

- When in the day are we seeing the child struggle? Is there a time-of-day pattern?

- Are we seeing a child struggle or need more support before or after a specific event?

Where?

- Where in the classroom or school do we see this type of situation or behavior?

- Where do we never or rarely see this type of situation or behavior? Does this give us clues?

With whom?

- Is there a pattern to who else is involved?

- Is there a pattern to who we never or rarely see involved?

How?

- How do the teachers typically respond? Is this response changing or lessening the behavior? Is the response meeting the child's underlying needs?

- How do the other children respond? Is this response changing or lessening the behavior? Is the response meeting the child's underlying needs?

- How does the situation resolve?

What?

- What is the child communicating through their behavior? Does the child have a need we can meet? Does the child need help learning a new skill? Does the child need us to change or adapt the classroom environment or curriculum?

Looking for patterns will allow us to develop a hypothesis or several hypotheses, depending on the child, that allow us to create our "best guesses" regarding the underlying needs expressed through the behaviors we observe in the classroom. Our understanding of development and the ways that trauma influences young children allows us to see the behavior from a trauma-informed lens. Once we understand the needs of the behavior, we can create a planned proactive approach to meet the needs of the child to lessen the behavior and build the child's felt sense of safety and trust. We can use the prevention strategies as well as the skill-building techniques discussed in this book to support the child in feeling accepted and safe in the classroom community.

Analyzing our observations and grouping them together into specific underlying needs allows us to see the children's behaviors for what they are: expressions of their internal states. With this information, we can then create ISPs that respond effectively to teach the children new skills and support them in feeling calm and safe.

Step Three: Create a Written Plan That Offers Consistent, Relationship-Based Interventions

Now that the ISP team has a better understanding of the child's specific needs, the team can write up a plan outlining the ways in which the child's needs can be addressed and supported in the classroom (Fulton and Macrossan 2008). The ISP can involve many of the strategies outlined in the previous chapters of this book: preventative techniques aimed at avoiding the challenging and baffling behaviors, educational skill-building opportunities, and effective relationship-based responses to elevate children's positive self-regard and sense of safety in the classroom.

For example, once we have gathered several observations of Josh, we may realize that his early food insecurity has him worried that there will not be enough snack for all the children, so when there is a food he particularly likes, he uses several different strategies to ensure he gets enough. Of course, there are many different strategies that could be used to support Josh in learning that there will always be food available, but his teachers chose these steps to try: (1) Snacktime will change from family style to individual servings of snack, with plenty of extra portions available for children who are still hungry. Josh will be reminded before snacktime begins that he can ask for more snack if he still feels hungry. The intent is for the child to no longer worry that he will not get any or that other children will eat all of the snack he wants; he will know that there is an individual portion waiting for him. (2) Healthy snacks, such as carrots, cucumbers, celery, apples, or bananas will always be available in the classroom. That way Josh can know when his set snacks or meals will be served, but if he is worried at all about feeling hungry or wondering if there will be enough food, he can always eat.

Once the initial ISP is created, those working with the child in the classroom can begin to implement their consistent and supportive approach.

Step Four: Reflect and Make Changes to the Written Plan as a Team

The process of scheduled and consistent reflection of the written plan ensures that the child's needs are continually met even as needs change throughout the year. As a child receives the nurturance, care, and attunement desperately needed to allow for a calm body and mind, the documented approaches may need to change as well. Every three to four weeks, review the ISP to get a sense of how the child is doing in the classroom and to see what changes, if any, need to be made to the plan. Here are some questions to be asked at the ISP review meeting:

- Has the plan contributed to a positive change for the child?

- Has the frequency of challenging or baffling behavior changed?

- Has the family continued to receive regular communication about what is occurring for their child?

- Have other professionals been involved? If so, how?

- Do some of the strategies not work? Should those strategies be removed from the plan?

- Do some of the strategies work well? Should similar strategies be added to the plan?

- What is going well for the child?

At this point in the process, the ISP team members may determine that a few of the strategies simply do not help the child or that the strategies are actually making things worse for the child. Reviewing the ISP every three to four weeks allows the teachers who work with the children directly to continue to grow their practice and modify and change their responses to children's trauma expressions.

Conclusion

By the time educators are working to build individualized support plans for children, frustrations may already be running high, and finding solutions can feel far from possible. However, with consistent response and implementation of ISPs, change can and does happen. Children who have experienced trauma deserve to feel included and supported at school. Their behaviors are showing us what is going on in their brains, and by understanding how their brains have been influenced by trauma, we can develop and incorporate strategies to help their brains heal.

Conclusion

CREATING TRAUMA-RESPONSIVE CLASSROOMS allows us to see beyond children's behaviors to understand their underlying needs; from a trauma-responsive perspective, their bodies tell us what their brains require to calm. It is our job as educators to respond to these needs in a way that helps children heal. To change children's personal narratives about their worth and expectations about safety and predictability, we must communicate that we see them and that they are loved. Through this complex and powerful work of deeply knowing and attuning to the children in our care, we can ensure that all children are valued and their contributions celebrated in our classrooms.

As trauma-responsive educators, we must continually reflect on our own practices, values, and biases as a means to adjust and improve our classroom environments and programs. By using a trauma-responsive lens to wonder about and analyze the challenging or baffling behaviors we see in the classroom, we are inevitably focusing greater attention on the quality of our interactions and relationships with all children and families. Through this process of looking beyond behavior, we are ensuring that children's social-emotional well-being is put at the forefront of our work, allowing us to be the supportive, loving, and appropriate adult figures all children deserve.

Understanding brain structure, attachment patterns, and development allows us to put aside our frustrations and confusions about children's actions and dig deep into understanding and responding to who they are. Having children who have experienced trauma in our classrooms allows us to modify and improve our teaching and classroom environment continually to ensure we are reaching all children in a way that is developmentally appropriate, honors the importance of inclusion, and values the pasts, presents, and futures of our children. As promoters of equity and justice, we must find ways to support all children because as trauma-responsive educators, we know that all children deserve safe and supportive classroom environments.

References

Auwarter, Amy, and Mara Aruguete. 2008. "Effects of Student Gender and Socioeconomic Status on Teacher Perceptions." *Journal of Educational Research* 101 (4): 243–46.

Badenoch, Bonnie. 2008. *Being a Brain-Wise Therapist: A Practical Guide to Interpersonal Neurobiology*. New York: W.W. Norton.

Barrett, Jennifer, and Alison Fleming. 2011. "Annual Research Review: All Mothers Are Not Created Equal: Neural and Psychobiological Perspectives on Mothering and the Importance of Individual Differences." *Journal of Child Psychology and Psychiatry* 52 (4): 368–97.

Bernheimer, Lily. 2019. *The Shaping of Us: How Everyday Spaces Structure Our Lives, Behaviour, and Well-Being*. San Antonio: Trinity University Press.

Blodgett, Christopher. 2014. "ACEs in Head Start Children and Impact on Development." Washington State University. https://s3.wp.wsu.edu/uploads/sites/2101/2019/12/ACEs-in-Head-Start-Children-and-Impact-on-Development-January-2014.pdf.

Blodgett, Christopher, and Jane Lanigan. 2018. "The Association between Adverse Childhood Experience (ACE) and School Success in Elementary School Children." *American Psychological Association* 33 (1): 137–46.

Bowlby, John. 1980. *Attachment and Loss*. Vol. 3, *Loss, Sadness, and Depression*. New York: Basic Books.

Budday, Silvia, Paul Steinmann, and Ellen Kuhl. 2014. "The Role of Mechanics during Brain Development." *Journal of the Mechanics and Physics of Solids* 72:75–92.

Burke Harris, Nadine. 2018. *The Deepest Well: Healing the Long-Term Effects of Childhood Adversity*. New York: Houghton Mifflin Harcourt.

Carter, Robert T. 2007. "Racism and Psychological and Emotional Injury: Recognizing and Assessing Race-Based Traumatic Stress." *Counseling Psychologist* 35 (1): 13–105.

Carter, Robert T., Michael Y. Lau, Veronica Johnson, and Katherine Kirkinis. 2017. "Racial Discrimination and Health Outcomes among Racial/Ethnic Minorities: A Meta-Analytic Review." *Journal of Multicultural Counseling and Development* 45 (4): 232–59.

Caspe, Margaret, Elena Lopez, and Rachel Hanebutt. 2019. "The Family Engagement Playbook." https://medium.com/familyengagementplaybook.

Chazin, Kate T., and Jennifer Ledford. 2016. "Challenging Behavior as Communication." *Evidence-Based Instructional Practices for Young Children with Autism and Other Disabilities*. http://ebip.vkcsites.org/challenging-behavior-as-communication.

Child Welfare Information Gateway. 2014a. "Parenting a Child Who Has Experienced Trauma." Washington, DC: U.S. Department of Health and Human Services, Children's Bureau.

———. 2014b. "Protective Factors: Approaches in Child Welfare." Washington, DC: U.S. Department of Health and Human Services, Children's Bureau.

———. 2015. "Understanding the Effects of Maltreatment on Brain Development." Washington, DC: U.S. Department of Health and Human Services, Children's Bureau.

———. 2016. "Racial Disproportionality and Disparity in Child Welfare." Washington, DC: U.S. Department of Health and Human Services, Children's Bureau.

connectABILITY. 2010. "ABC functional assessment card." https://connectability.ca /2010/09/23/abc-functional-assessment-card.

Cook, Alexandra, Margaret Blaustein, Joseph Spinazzola, and Bessel van der Kolk, eds. 2003. "Complex Trauma in Children and Adolescents." *National Child Traumatic Stress Network*. https://www.nctsn.org/resources/complex-trauma-children-and-adolescents.

D'Andrea, Wendy, Julian Ford, Bradley Stolbach, Joseph Spinazzola, and Bessel A. van der Kolk. 2012. "Understanding Interpersonal Trauma in Children: Why We Need a Developmentally Appropriate Trauma Diagnosis." *American Journal of Orthopsychiatry* 82:187–200.

De Bellis, Michael D., and Abigail A. Zisk. 2014. "The Biological Effects of Childhood Trauma." *Child and Adolescent Psychiatric Clinics of North America* 23 (2): 185–222.

Dell'Antonia, KJ. 2014. "The New Inequality for Toddlers: Less Income; More Ritalin." *New York Times*. May 16, 2014. http://parenting.blogs.nytimes.com/2014/05/16/the-new -inequality-for-toddlers-less-income-more-ritalin.

Duplechain, Rosalind, Ronald Reigner, and Abbot Packard. 2008. "Striking Differences: The Impact of Moderate and High Trauma on Reading Achievement." *Reading Psychology* 29 (2): 117–36.

Dwyer, Jenny, Judy O'Keefe, Paul Scott, and Lauren Wilson. 2012. "Literature Review: A Trauma-Sensitive Approach for Children Aged 0–8 Years." Trauma and Young Children —a Caring Approach Project Women's Health Goulburn. https://www.whealth.com.au /documents/work/trauma/LiteratureReview.pdf.

Felitti, Vincent J., Robert F. Anda, Dale Nordenberg, David F. Williamson, Alison M. Spitz, Valerie Edwards, Mary Koss, and James S. Marks. 1998. "Relationship of Childhood Abuse and Household Dysfunction to Many of the Leading Causes of Death in Adults: The Adverse Childhood Experiences (ACE) Study." *American Journal of Preventive Medicine* 14 (4): 245–58.

Florez, Ida Rose. 2011. "Developing Young Children's Self-Regulation through Everyday Experiences." *Young Children* 66 (4): 46–51.

Fulton, Elizabeth, and Pam Macrossan. 2008. "Developing Individualised Behaviour Plans That Promote a Child's Social and Emotional Development and Protect the Safety and Well-Being of All Children and Adults in Early Childhood Settings." Paper presented at the Early Childhood Australia Conference, October 2008.

Gaskill, Richard L., and Bruce D. Perry. 2014. "The Neurobiological Power of Play: Using the Neurosequential Model of Therapeutics to Guide Play in the Healing Process." In *Creative Arts and Play Therapy for Attachment Problems*, edited by Cathy A. Malchiodi and David A. Crenshaw, 178–94. New York: The Guilford Press.

Gerber, Magda, and Allison Johnson. 1998. *Your Self-Confident Baby: How to Encourage Your Child's Natural Abilities—from the Very Start.* New York: John Wiley and Sons.

Gilliam, Walter S. 2005. "Prekindergartners Left Behind: Expulsion Rates in State Prekindergarten Systems." *Foundation for Child Development Policy Brief No. 3.* New Haven, CT: Yale University Child Study Center.

———. 2008. "Implementing Policies to Reduce the Likelihood of Preschool Expulsion." *Foundation for Child Development Policy Brief No. 7.* New Haven, CT: Yale University Child Study Center.

Gilliam, Walter, Angela N. Maupin, Chin R. Reyes, Maria Accavitti, and Frederick Shic. 2016. "Do Early Educators' Implicit Biases Regarding Sex and Race Relate to Behavior Expectations and Recommendations of Preschool Expulsions and Suspensions?" *A Research Study Brief.* New Haven, CT: Yale University Child Study Center.

Gray, Deborah D. 2012. *Nurturing Adoptions: Creating Resilience after Neglect and Trauma.* London: Jessica Kingsley Publishers.

Hartley, Catherine A., and Francis S. Lee. 2014. "Sensitive Periods in Affective Development: Nonlinear Maturation of Fear Learning." *Neuropsychopharmacology* 40:50–60.

Harvey, Mary R. 1996. "An Ecological View of Psychological Trauma and Trauma Recovery." *Journal of Traumatic Stress* 9 (1): 3–23.

Hassinger-Das, Brenna, Kathy Hirsh-Pasek, and Roberta Michnick Golinkoff. 2017. "The Case of Brain Science and Guided Play: A Developing Story." *Young Children* 72 (2): 45–50.

Head Start Bulletin. 2009. "Mental Health (Issue 80)." Washington, DC: Office of Head Start, Administration for Children and Families, U.S. Department of Health and Human Services.

Hemmings, Carrie, and Amanda M. Evans. 2017. "Identifying and Treating Race-Based Trauma in Counseling." *Journal of Multicultural Counseling and Development* 46:20–39.

HHS (U.S. Department of Health and Human Services, Administration for Children and Families, Administration on Children, Youth and Families, Children's Bureau). 2020. "Child Maltreatment 2018." Accessed January 2020. www.acf.hhs.gov/sites/default/files/cb/cm2018.pdf.

Holmes, Cheryl, Michelle Levy, Avis Smith, Susan Pinne, and Paula Neese. 2014. "A Model for Creating a Supportive Trauma-Informed Culture for Children in Preschool Settings." *Journal of Child and Family Studies* 24:1650–59.

Isobel, Sophie, Melinda Goodyear, Trentham Furness, and Kim Foster. 2018. "Preventing Intergenerational Trauma Transmission: A Critical Interpretive Synthesis." *Journal of Clinical Nursing* 28:1100–13.

Jimenez, Manuel E., Roy Wade Jr., Yong Lin, Lesley M. Morrow, and Nancy E. Reichman. 2016. "Adverse Experiences in Early Childhood and Kindergarten Outcomes." *Pediatrics* 137 (2): 1–9.

Joseph, Gail E., Phil Strain, Tweety Yates, and Mary Louise Hemmeter. 2010. "Social Emotional Teaching Strategies." The Center on the Social and Emotional Foundations for Early Learning.

Manning, Brittany L., Megan Y. Roberts, Ryne Estabrook, Amélie Petitclerc, James L. Burns, Margaret Briggs-Gowan, Lauren S. Wakschlag, and Elizabeth S. Norton. 2019. "Relations between Toddler Expressive Language and Temper Tantrums in a Community Sample." *Journal of Applied Developmental Psychology* 65:101070.

Marchetti, Letha. 2015. *Dragons and Daisies: Keys to Resolve Baffling Behaviors in Early Childhood Education.* OT Home Services.

Marvin, Rovert, Glen Cooper, Kent Hoffman, and Bert Powell. 2002. "The Circle of Security Project: Attachment-Based Intervention with Caregiver-Pre-School Child Dyads." *Attachment & Human Development* 4 (1): 107–24.

McCrory, Eamon J., Stephane A. De Brito, and Essi Viding. 2010. "Research Review: The Neurobiology and Genetics of Maltreatment and Adversity." *Journal of Child Psychology and Psychiatry* 51:1079–95.

Mesman, Judi, Marinus H. van Ijzendoorn, and Marian J. Bakermans-Kranenburg. 2009. "The Many Faces of the Still-Face Paradigm: A Review and Meta-Analysis." *Developmental Review* 29 (2): 120–62.

Moon, Christine, Randall C. Zernzach, and Patricia K. Kuhl. 2015. "Mothers Say 'Baby' and Their Newborns Do Not Choose to Listen: A Behavioral Preference Study to Compare with ERP Results." *Frontiers in Human Neuroscience* 9:86–91.

Moore, Jan. 2013. "Research Summary: Resilience and At-Risk Children and Youth." National Center for Homeless Education. https://nche.ed.gov/wp-content/uploads /2018/11/resilience.pdf.

National Scientific Council on the Developing Child. 2004. "Children's Emotional Development Is Built into the Architecture of Their Brains: Working Paper No. 2." Cambridge, MA: Center on the Developing Child at Harvard University.

———. 2008. "Mental Health Problems in Early Childhood Can Impair Learning and Behavior for Life: Working Paper No. 6." Cambridge, MA: Center on the Developing Child at Harvard University.

———. 2010a. "Persistent Fear and Anxiety Can Affect Young Children's Learning and Development: Working Paper No. 9." Cambridge, MA: Center on the Developing Child at Harvard University.

———. 2010b. "Early Experiences Can Alter Gene Expression and Affect Long-Term Development: Working Paper No. 10." Cambridge, MA: Center of the Developing Child at Harvard University.

———. 2011. "Building the Brain's 'Air Traffic Control' System: How Early Experiences Shape the Development of Executive Function: Working Paper No. 11." Cambridge, MA: Center on the Developing Child at Harvard University.

———. 2012. "The Science of Neglect: The Persistent Absence of Responsive Care Disrupts the Developing Brain: Working Paper No. 12." Cambridge, MA: Center on the Developing Child at Harvard University.

———. 2014. "Excessive Stress Disrupts the Architecture of the Developing Brain: Working Paper No. 3, Updated Edition." Cambridge, MA: Center on the Developing Child at Harvard University.

———. 2015. "Supportive Relationships and Active Skill-Building Strengthen the Foundations of Resilience: Working Paper No. 13." Cambridge, MA: Center on the Developing Child at Harvard University.

NCTSN (National Child Traumatic Stress Network). 2014. "Complex Trauma: Facts for Educators." Los Angeles, CA, and Durham, NC: National Center for Child Traumatic Stress.

———. 2017. "Addressing Race and Trauma in the Classroom: A Resource for Educators." Los Angeles, CA, and Durham, NC: National Center for Child Traumatic Stress.

Newman, Louise, Carmel Sivaratnam, and Angela Komiti. 2015. "Attachment and Early Brain Development—Neuroprotective Interventions in Infant-Caregiver Therapy." *Translational Developmental Psychiatry* 3 (1): 28647. https://doi.org/10.3402/tdp.v3.28647.

Peterson, Karen L. 2014. *Helping Them Heal: How Teachers Can Support Young Children Who Experience Stress and Trauma.* Lewisville, NC: Gryphon House.

Plumb, Jacqui L., Kelly A. Bush, and Sonia E. Kersevich. 2016. "Trauma-Sensitive Schools: An Evidence-Based Approach." *School Social Work Journal* 40 (2): 37–60.

Purvis, Karyn B., David R. Cross, Donald F. Dansereau, and Sheri R. Parris. 2013. "Trust-Based Relational Intervention (TBRI): A Systematic Approach to Complex Developmental Trauma." *Child and Youth Services* 24:360–86.

Resnick, Michael D., and Lindsay A. Taliaferro. 2012. "Resilience." In *Encyclopedia of Adolescence,* edited by B. Bradford Brown and Mitchell J. Prinstein, 299–306. San Diego: Academic Press.

Roberts, Andrea L., Margaret Rosario, Heather L. Corliss, Karestan C. Koenen, and S. Bryn Austin. 2012. "Childhood Gender Nonconformity: A Risk Indicator for Childhood Abuse and Posttraumatic Stress in Youth." *Pediatrics* 129 (3): 410–17.

Ruiz, Rebecca. 2014. "How Childhood Trauma Could Be Mistaken for ADHD: Some Experts Say the Normal Effects of Severe Adversity May Be Misdiagnosed as ADHD." *Atlantic*. Accessed January 2020. https://www.theatlantic.com/health/archive/2014/07/how -childhood-trauma-could-be-mistaken-for-adhd/373328.

Saigh, Philip A., Anastasia E. Yasik, Richard A. Oberfield, Phill V. Halamandaris, and J. Douglas Bremner. 2006. "The Intellectual Performance of Traumatized Children and Adolescents with or without Posttraumatic Stress Disorder." *Journal of Abnormal Psychology* 115 (2): 332–40.

SAMHSA (Substance Abuse and Mental Health Services Administration). 2012. *Supporting Infants, Toddlers, and Families Impacted by Caregiver Mental Health Problems, Substance Abuse, and Trauma, A Community Action Guide. DHHS Publication No. SMA-12-4726*. Rockville, MD: Substance Abuse and Mental Health Services Administration.

———. 2014. *SAMHSA's Concept of Trauma and Guidance for a Trauma-Informed Approach. HHS Publication No. (SMA) 14-4884*. Rockville, MD: Substance Abuse and Mental Health Services Administration.

Schore, Allan N. 2003. *Affect Dysregulation and Disorders of the Self*. New York: W.W. Norton.

Schwartz, Alan. 2014. "Thousands of Toddlers Are Medicated for A.D.H.D., Report Finds, Raising Worries." *New York Times*, May 17, 2014. http://www.nytimes.com/2014/05/17 /us/among-experts-scrutiny-of-attention-disorder-diagnoses-in-2-and-3-year-olds .html.

Scott, Brandon G., Nadine J. Burke, Carl F. Weems, Julia L. Hellman, and Victor G. Carrión. 2013. "The Interrelation of Adverse Childhood Experiences within an At-Risk Pediatric Sample." *Journal of Child and Adolescent Trauma* 6:217–29.

Seibel, Nancy L., Donna Britt, Linda G. Gillespie, and Rebecca Parlakian. 2006. "Preventing Child Abuse and Neglect: Parent-Provider Partnerships in Child Care." Washington, DC: ZERO TO THREE Press.

Shonkoff, Jack P., and Deborah A. Phillips, eds. 2000. *From Neurons to Neighborhoods: The Science of Early Childhood Development*. Washington DC: National Academy Press.

Siegel, Daniel J., and Tina Payne Bryson. 2011. *The Whole-Brain Child: 12 Revolutionary Strategies to Nurture Your Child's Developing Mind*. New York: Delacorte Press.

Siegfried, Christine B., and Kimberly L. Blackshear. 2016. "Is It ADHD or Child Traumatic Stress? A Guide for Clinicians." Los Angeles, CA, and Durham, NC: National Center for Child Traumatic Stress.

Souers, Kristin, and Pete Hall. 2016. *Fostering Resilient Learners: Strategies for Creating a Trauma-Sensitive Classroom*. Alexandria, VA: ASCD.

Spratt, Eve G., Samantha L. Friedenberg, Cynthia C. Swenson, Angela LaRosa, Michael D. De Bellis, Michelle M. Macias, Andrea P. Summer, Thomas C. Hulsey, Des K. Runyan, and Kathleen T. Brady. 2012. "The Effects of Early Neglect on Cognitive, Language, and Behavioral Functioning in Childhood." *Psychology* 3:175–82.

Stephens, Ruth. 2018. "Sensory Processing, Coordination and Attachment." Beacon House Therapeutic Services and Trauma Team. https://beaconhouse.org.uk/useful-resources.

Stock Kranowitz, Carol. 2006. *The Out-of-Sync Child: Recognizing and Coping with Sensory Processing Disorder*. New York: TarcherPerigree.

Sylvestre, Audette, Eve-Line Bussières, and Caroline Bouchard. 2015. "Language Problems among Abused and Neglected Children: A Meta-Analytic Review." *Child Maltreatment* 21 (1): 47–58.

Teicher, Martin, Jacqueline Samson, Carl Anderson, and Kyoko Ohashi. 2016. "The Effects of Childhood Maltreatment on Brain Structure, Function and Connectivity." *Nature Reviews Neuroscience* 17 (10): 652–66.

Thomason, Moriah E., and Hilary A. Marusak. 2017. "Toward Understanding the Impact of Trauma on the Early Developing Human Brain." *Neuroscience* 342:55–67.

van der Kolk, Bessel. 2014. *The Body Keeps the Score: Brain, Mind, and Body in the Healing of Trauma*. New York: Penguin Books.

Vanderbilt-Adriance, Ella, and Daniel S. Shaw. 2008. "Protective Factors and the Development of Resilience in the Context of Neighborhood Disadvantage." *Journal of Abnormal Child Psychology* 36 (6): 887–901.

Vygotsky, Lev S. 1978. *Mind in Society: The Development of Higher Psychological Processes*. Cambridge, MA: Harvard University Press.

Zero to Six Collaborative Group, NCTSN (National Child Traumatic Stress Network). 2010. "Early Childhood Trauma." Los Angeles, CA, and Durham, NC: National Center for Child Traumatic Stress.

Zhang, Wei, J. Finik, Kathryn Dana, Vivette Glover, Jacob Ham, and Yoko Nomura. 2018. "Prenatal Depression and Infant Temperament: The Moderating Role of Placental Gene Expression." *Infancy* 23:211–31.

Index